Creating Opera Utilising Augmented Reality and Virtual Reality Technologies

This book investigates the use of extended reality (XR) technologies to innovate the opera experience.

Through the creation and comparison of three versions of the original opera Artemis, the research explores how virtual and augmented reality platforms can transform traditional composition and staging practices. The project resulted in three distinct iterations: a virtual reality opera built in Unity3D for the Oculus Quest, a 360° YouTube VR opera, and an augmented reality live performance. Each version utilised self-experiential prototyping to craft immersive environments and novel compositional approaches. Key features of this book include a detailed analysis of prototyping methods for XR opera development, with an emphasis on combining autoethnography, world-building, and user-centric design. By leveraging tools like Unity3D and 3D spatial sound technology, the research demonstrates how XR environments can enhance the sensory and emotional engagement of both creators and audiences. Readers will gain practical insights into designing XR operas, from managing technical constraints to creating immersive soundscapes and environments that align with operatic narratives.

This book will appeal to an academic audience in fields such as music technology, interaction design, composition, and virtual reality architecture. It provides valuable contributions for undergraduate and postgraduate students, creative practice researchers, and professionals seeking to explore the intersections of technology, performance, and composition. With its multidisciplinary approach, this book offers a roadmap for applying innovative techniques to the creation of XR operatic works and beyond.

Taana Rose is a guest lecturer at TAFE Queensland with a PhD from the University of Queensland. Having taught autoethnography, music for screen, composition, music technology, and sound design at TAFE Queensland and The University of Canberra, she also tutors Indigenous students through the Keystones of Success program, at the Queensland University of Technology. She has graced prestigious stages like GameSoundCon, Highscore 2022, and EUROXR, showcasing her expertise in immersive soundscapes and XR innovation. Creator of the mesmerising Artemis XR Opera and the acclaimed Artemis VR, Taana's work has reached global audiences, earning her the esteemed Best in Queensland Award at QLDXRFestival 2022. As a sound designer, she has added her sonic magic to the VR experience 'Allegory of Reality', showcased at Vacant Assembly and World Science Festival Brisbane.

Creating Opera Utilising Augmented Reality and Virtual Reality Technologies

Taana Rose

LONDON AND NEW YORK

First published 2025
by Routledge
4 Park Square, Milton Park, Abingdon, Oxon OX14 4RN

and by Routledge
605 Third Avenue, New York, NY 10158

Routledge is an imprint of the Taylor & Francis Group, an informa business

© 2025 Taana Rose

The right of Taana Rose to be identified as author of this work has been asserted in accordance with sections 77 and 78 of the Copyright, Designs and Patents Act 1988.

All rights reserved. No part of this book may be reprinted or reproduced or utilised in any form or by any electronic, mechanical, or other means, now known or hereafter invented, including photocopying and recording, or in any information storage or retrieval system, without permission in writing from the publishers.

Trademark notice: Product or corporate names may be trademarks or registered trademarks, and are used only for identification and explanation without intent to infringe.

British Library Cataloguing-in-Publication Data
A catalogue record for this book is available from the British Library

ISBN: 9781041077183 (hbk)
ISBN: 9781041077190 (pbk)
ISBN: 9781003642541 (ebk)

DOI: 10.4324/9781003642541

Typeset in Times New Roman
by codeMantra

Contents

List of Figures	*vii*
List of Tables	*ix*
About the Author	*xi*
Acknowledgements	*xiii*
List of Abbreviations	*xv*
Overview	*xvii*
1 Introduction	1
2 Thematic Context	9
3 Review of Relevant Artworks	14
4 Voicing Artemis	28
5 A Comparison of the AR and VR *Artemis* Works	36
6 Prototyping an Iterative Process	48
7 The Composer, as Maker	70
Appendices	*77*
References	*89*
Index	*99*

Figures

1.1	A flow chart of my cyclic reflective process	6
4.1	Artemis with a Stag. Statue housed in the Louvre Museum. First or second century AD. Copy of a lost Greek bronze by Leochares, circa 325BC. Image by rjhuttondfw. Creative Commons – Attribution 2.0 Generic – CC BY 2.0. No changes made. [https://www.flickr.com/photos/rjhuttondfw/10678561295/in/photolist-2mBq3ZA-5hWYJJ-hgCqeM-8jVwdb-a9V7dq-3aY25-nZELcw]	29
4.2	Limestone statue of the goddess Artemis housed at the MET. MET public domain image	30
4.3	Artemis housed in the Vatican Museum. Image by rjhuttondfw. Creative Commons – Attribution – ShareAlike 2.0 Generic - CC BY-SA 2.0. No changes made. [https://www.flickr.com/photos/rjhuttondfw/20654213895]	31
5.1	Screenshots of the YouTube VR Artemis version (26 December 2021 iteration)	38
5.2	Target images and QR code screenshots for the AR version of Artemis	43
6.1	My self-experiential prototyping: an iterative cyclic model	51
6.2	Structured and sequential self-experiential process steps for Oculus Quest prototyping	52
6.3	Process of music prototyping for XR	63
6.4	Process of audio post-production for XR	64
6.5	Process of prototyping for Oculus VR	65
6.6	Process of prototyping for YouTube VR	67
6.7	Process of prototyping for AR	68
6.8	Venn diagram showing the overlaps in the creation process	69

Tables

5.1	User Roles Across a Spectrum of Interactivity	42
6.1	Journal Entries for the Oculus VR Iterations	55
7.1	Dolan Paret's Framework for VR Storytelling	72

About the Author

Taana Rose is a guest lecturer at TAFE Queensland with a PhD from the University of Queensland. Having taught autoethnography, music for screen, composition, music technology, and sound design at TAFE Queensland and The University of Canberra, she tutors Indigenous students through the Keystones of Success program, at the Queensland University of Technology. She has graced prestigious stages like GameSoundCon, Highscore 2022, and EUROXR, showcasing her expertise in immersive soundscapes and XR innovation. Creator of the mesmerising Artemis XR Opera and the acclaimed Artemis VR, Taana's work has reached global audiences, earning her the esteemed Best in Queensland Award at QLDXRFestival 2022. As a sound designer, she has added her sonic magic to the VR experience 'Allegory of Reality', showcased at Vacant Assembly and World Science Festival Brisbane.

Acknowledgements

Thank you to Lucie Bartonek of Routledge, Taylor & Francis. Thank you to editorial assistant Nabila Khadija Ansari of Routledge, Taylor & Francis. Thank you to Evie Evans of Routledge, Taylor & Francis UK.

I would not be the composer, VR creator, and technologist that I am today without the help of my supervisors and mentors. I would like to express my immense gratitude to my primary PhD supervisor, Dr Eve Klein, for supporting me throughout my PhD journey. Her encouragement, always helpful feedback, expert advice, continued enthusiasm, and fortnightly meetings were of tremendous help. I also wish to thank my associate PhD supervisor, Dr Fred Fialho Teixeira, for his digital architecture expertise, Unity3D advice, helpful meetings, and feedback. I am grateful to my mentor, Michelle Brown, for the VR lessons and for hiring me to create the sound design for Allegory of Reality.

I am very grateful to the University of Queensland for allowing me to compose and produce the 2020 BLOOM Festival Light and Sound Display soundtrack and to use my Artemis XR Opera as a partner performance at the UQ BLOOM Festival 2022.

This research would not have been possible without my fantastic collaborators, Luisa Tarnawski, Connor Willmore, Jasmine Buckley, Melfred Lijauco, and Nick Kirkup, who brilliantly workshopped and performed my opera.

Abbreviations

AR	Augmented reality
VR	Virtual reality
XR	Extended reality
UI	User interface
UX	User experience
HCI	Human computer interaction
VE	Virtual environment

Overview

The research questions explored in this book are: How can self-experiential prototyping methodologies be used to create new opera experiences? Second, what can be learnt by comparing three AR and VR opera creation processes based on the same operatic source material? The problem statement investigated is: How can a maker use self-experiential prototyping to create a new XR opera? The gap in the literature and the gap in the knowledge where I situated this study was creating XR opera from a self-experiential maker perspective.

Where I was leading with this research was, firstly, the blurring of music and visual roles to become a multidisciplinary creator, explored through autoethnographic research. Secondly, I created experiences where the audience became a user rather than merely a spectator, as audience members usually are passive spectators at traditional Western classical opera performances. I achieved these two caveats by composing an opera for different formats. I pulled from the tech world of user experience design (UX) for my methodology as I developed my prototyping techniques and models. My research was about reaching broader audiences. Thus, the methodology did not use user studies. My study was about something other than user testing, as I honed in on being a maker from the outset rather than exploring user testing, audience observation, or audience experience. The demographics of each experience are as follows: The YouTube VR version was created for people at home during the COVID-19 pandemic, which impacted my compositional decisions (both musical and visual) in designing the experience.

Similarly, in the AR experience, I had the Nickson Room live performance in mind from the outset, and this impacted my compositional decisions (both musical and visual) in designing the experience. Future avenues of research include adaptive audio in gaming. Further, immersion research needs to include user testing or psychological testing, which I did not get around to in this study. Thus, this could be future work. In this research project, I set out to document the creation of an XR opera using self-experiential prototyping. The point of departure was researching from a maker's perspective and incorporating the tech side of prototyping into a music composition book. I departed from traditional opera by creating a multidisciplinary book that combined music technology, digital opera, and prototyping techniques.

1 Introduction

1.1 Introduction

This book is set out into chapters that highlight key elements in XR creation and design.

Chapter 1 looks at the methodology and background of the creative folio and research, outlining my background as a researcher and the underpinning inspiration for the research. Chapter 2 looks at the literature behind the various concepts explored in the written and creative works; Chapter 2 outlines how my research was influenced by prior research in VR, AR, XR, and immersive theatre. I also discuss this book's thematic context in Chapter 2. Chapter 3 reviews relevant artworks, delves deeper into relevant creative works and opera content, and discusses how they relate to my research. Chapter 4 outlines how opera was inspired by Greek mythology. I explore various archetypes and interpretations of the Greek goddess Artemis throughout history. In Chapter 5, I compare my AR and VR works through the lens of experience, discussing the lessons learned and their implications. Chapter 6 delves into the specific prototyping processes utilised in the creation of the XR opera, *Artemis*. In Chapter 7, I present the conclusions drawn through the lens of a composer as a maker.

This research aimed to innovate opera using extended reality (XR)[1] by comparing three versions of an originally produced and composed opera in different mediums; these three versions encompassed a virtual reality opera constructed in *Unity3D* (*see* media example 19), a 360° YouTube VR (*see* media example 18) opera, and an augmented reality (AR) opera performance (see media example 05). Each version was a reconfiguration of an original traditionally composed opera, *Artemis* (*see* media example 33 *and* media example 34). These three opera versions were used as comparative case studies to examine how self-experiential prototyping processes shape the creation of new XR opera. By comparing these creation processes, I sought to fill a knowledge gap through self-experiential prototyping. Self-experiential prototyping for XR opera making has not previously been attempted in the context of a research project. My work explores self-experiential prototyping processes from an autoethnographic and educational standpoint, which is novel.

DOI: 10.4324/9781003642541-1

Students can watch the additional tutorial content that accompanies this book at: https://taanarosemusic.weebly.com/phd-portfolio-walkthrough-videos.html

This book examines my *Artemis* XR opera in detail through discussions of effective prototyping techniques and implementation. I consider how autoethnography can be used for successful prototyping and how the design and implementation underpinning the creative development process for virtual environments can be used to stage my new *Artemis* XR opera. Creating an XR opera requires the creator to be multidisciplinary (Nitschke, 2018a, b). Creating the virtual environment for *Artemis* brought together game design, architecture, game aesthetics, broad-brush prototyping, and precision to create a comfortable and safe user experience.

I used Unity3D, a platform for 3D world creation, to create an Oculus VR version of the opera work for Oculus Quest. I designed a world that enhances the word painting of each opera piece. This combination of word painting (McClanahan, 1999) and world-building immerses the creator and audience both sonically and visually. Peters, Heijligers, Kievith, Razafindrakoto, Van Oosterhout, Santos, Mayer, and Louwerse (2016) found that Unity3D was the most adaptable and robust software for VR and AR applications, which seems to correlate with present-day industry usage.

In this book, I describe the techniques used to increase the effectiveness of XR opera prototyping, including 3D spatial sound as an inexpensive user interface (UI) aid for graphics trade-off (Laurel, 2013). I employed 3D spatial sound in my Oculus prototype development using the Unity3D spatialiser plugin to map audio to assets. I learnt from this how to best use proximity to trigger audio events in Unity3D (see media example 25, media example 26, media example 27).

1.2 Relevance and Research Questions

I experimented with painting the virtual environment models for the Oculus VR experience in Tilt Brush and importing my Tilt Brush painting into Unity3D with the Poly software kit, editing the virtual world in Unity3D, and distributing it on Oculus Quest to be experienced with Oculus Link throughout the prototyping. The learnings I present in this book include self-experiential prototyping methodologies and models and the creative processes I employed as a composer-designer. These learnings may be helpful for composer-designers who are looking to create their own XR productions.

Australian opera is changing, highlighting the need to explore methods of opera creation using XR and immersive technologies. This research is timely because opera companies increasingly seek to create immersive and XR opera experiences, and opera's engagement with technology is generally increasing (National Opera Review, Australian Government report, 2016). In the Australian context, this impetus is reflected in the recommendations of the National Opera Review (2016), which emphasised the need to 'support the presentation of innovative works in collaboration with festivals' (p. 54) and 'increase the use of digital technology for innovation' (p. 55). Following these recommendations, Opera Australia has prioritised the digital staging of opera works by launching a new production of *The Ring Cycle* (Wagner, 1857). The former artistic director of Opera Australia modernised opera by including new technologies, such as digital sets and projection screens (Cockburn, 2022, October 6); this can be seen further in Opera Queensland's AR rendition of *The Magic Flute* (Mozart, 1791) as a prototype app called *Project AR-ia* showcased at Siggraph 2019.

Outside Australia, the *Current, Rising* (Fernando, 2020) production at the Royal Opera House shows a similar move towards 'hyperreality'.[2] Moreover, opera companies have utilised AR or VR to engage new and younger audiences by reimagining old works. Examples are the Welsh National Opera's *Magic Butterfly* VR (2017) production and *A Little Vixen* (2019) and Javornik, Rogers, Gander, and Moutinho's (2017) MagicFace app. Opera companies are also creating new works, such as White Snake Projects' virtual video game opera *PermaDeath*, composed by Dan Visconti (2018), which combines the sound world of video games with opera. The staged mixed-reality techno-opera *Maya* (Nitschke, 2018) and Tapestry Opera also use XR technologies. Thus, given the rapid adoption of XR technologies into opera, it is likely that future directions in opera will include the constant incorporation of XR technologies into new productions, and composers will need to be comfortable creating compositional work that integrates XR mediums. To explore the terrain of XR opera exploration, I arrived at two research questions. I chose these two research questions as they are innovative and have not been researched before; thus, this study sought to answer the following questions: How can self-experiential prototyping methodologies be used to create new opera experiences? What can be learnt by comparing three AR and VR opera creation processes based on the same operatic source material? These questions are important as they fill a gap in the literature through action research. The gap is self-experiential prototyping of XR visuals and music prototyping.

1.3 Context and Background

My research emerged from my background as an acoustic singer-songwriter. I learned how to be an electronic music producer, performer, and sound engineer during my undergraduate studies. I then combined electronics with classical composition during my master's degree, where I studied electro-acoustic composition. Throughout my master's studies, I was inspired by XR works at art exhibitions, live opera productions, and concerts that I frequently watched at the UQ School of Music, Queensland Performing Arts Centre, and the Queensland Conservatorium of Music, Griffith University. This research project was motivated by my desire to fuse my technological and compositional backgrounds and combine them with my love for opera. Due to my experience in merging composition with new technologies, this project is built on my previous compositional practice as an electro-acoustic and opera composer and music technologist. Thus, I am well-positioned to address this project's research questions.

My portfolio consisted of two works, *Artemis* and *Flourishing Hope*. *Artemis* is represented in three distinct forms. The first form is an interactive AR opera production in which users interact with the live performance using a smartphone application that scans QR codes to display AR content (see media example 05). The second form is a Unity3D VR production. Users experience the opera using a mobile Oculus Quest VR headset, walking through the virtual world to listen to the opera (see media example 19). The third form is 360° YouTube VR content, experienced by wearing VR goggles and walking around a pre-rendered 360° world (see media example 18).

The opera tells the story of Artemis, the Greek goddess of the wilderness. *Artemis* comprises four movements for classical and electronic instrumentation: mezzo-soprano, tenor, piano, and synthesiser. The XR opera contains a composition for each season of Artemis's life (birth, adolescence, middle age, and later years). 'Licht und Liebe' is a metaphor for Artemis's birth, whilst 'Mi amor la luna' represents her adolescence and summer. Autumn is a summary of her midlife, in which she sings 'Autumn ayre da capo aria'. 'Winter Duet' symbolises the final season of her life. These are presented in non-linear order, beginning with the spring birth duet 'Licht und Liebe' and moving to 'Winter Duet', where Artemis's lover Orion dies. 'Autumn ayre da capo aria' and 'Mi amor la luna' are performed. I chose to present the opera in this order as flashbacks, drawing upon narrative design to create the experience, drawing upon Bucher (2018) for the best ways to structure virtual reality experiences and best practices for VR storytelling.

I developed the Oculus prototype of *Artemis* in Unity3D simultaneously with the interactive opera composition, which I wrote using Finale (Western notation scoring software). I experimented with implementing the composition in the Unity3D environment with audio middleware.[3] However, I decided to put the audio files directly into the Unity3D game engine for the final Oculus VR version, the learning for me as it related to my research was that Unity3D has helpful game audio implementation; I increased my skill set to be a game developer and game audio implementer (see media example 27).

The portfolio addendum work, *Flourishing Hope*, is an immersive experience created for the UQ BLOOM Festival 2020 (see media example 01). This work, documented through archival footage, provides an instrumental music case study that can be compared to the operatic compositional process (see media example 02). *Flourishing Hope* is an example of a light and sound installation outside the operatic form. The BLOOM Festival *Flourishing Hope* experience was my first composition for a light display in front of a massive public audience (see media example 03); I incorporated the learnings gleaned from composing for this experience into the opera works (see media example 04).

This book addresses the research questions to explore the self-experiential prototyping process of XR opera creation. Thematic context and a review of relevant artworks of seminal XR and non-linear works provide the background and foundation of what is explored. This book is divided into seven chapters concerning various aspects of XR opera creation.

1.4 Aim

Finessing an audio experience in 3D environments was what I hoped to achieve. Therefore, this research focused on developing effective interactive composition techniques applied to the operatic form in XR environments. I developed the research process through the making of each experience, gaining learnings from recreating the same operatic text in different mediums, and then reflecting upon the challenges and opportunities of adaptation.

1.5 Assets Defined

Some versions of *Artemis* presented in this book use pre-made assets. An asset is a 3D model that can be downloaded and added to a Unity3D project. Using assets is a normal part of the game development process, similar to using stock footage or images (Goldstone, 2009). I designed and built the virtual world using pre-made assets from the Unity3D (Unity Technologies, 2022) store, Tilt Brush Poly models, and self-painted Tilt Brush FBX assets.

1.6 Conceptual Framework

I conducted practice-based research throughout my PhD studies to develop my creative portfolio and craft the compositions. To develop this book, I used autoethnography and practice-based research. The triangulation (Silverman, 2017) of these methods created a cohesive research framework. Throughout this research project, I explored how self-experiential prototyping methodologies can be used to create new opera experiences. I used different technologies to create a new XR opera form. My research drew upon Smith and Dean's (2009) model of the iterative web of practice-led research and Candy's (2006) conceptualisation of practice-based research.

According to Smith and Dean (2009), research and creative practice converge. Research insights can be gained by crafting creative work and theorising on it. Thus, practice and research interact in a continuous cycle. However, research can also result in creative practice, creating a 'cyclic web'. Practice-led research and research-led practice are not separate entities but are fluid processes that create new knowledge. Smith and Dean argue that artworks transmit knowledge. This knowledge is communicated non-verbally and non-numerically. Smith and Dean (2009) also argued that research can include the development and creation of sonic artwork. The term 'research' should be sufficiently flexible to accommodate a research project's fundamental, continuous, and cyclic nature. Therefore, research leads to creative practice, and academic knowledge may lead out of one's creative practice. At the same time, practice-led research is related to conventional qualitative and quantitative research and should not be divorced from these methods.

According to Candy (2006), practice-based research is a creative product combined with the written word. In practice-based research, creative work is the research, whereas in practice-led research, one does not need a creative outcome (Candy, 2006). Thus, my research is practice-based (Figure 1.1).

In this work, I implemented a cyclic reflective process of idea generation through my models and iterative methodology to answer research question 1, 'How can self-experiential prototyping methodologies be used to create new opera experiences?'

The output is the artwork *Artemis* created through the development of selected ideas, as well as the documentation of the artwork, and its production consists of my website walk-through videos, video documentation, and a written book. The research-led practice component is the application of theories

Figure 1.1 A flow chart of my cyclic reflective process.

and techniques to new creative work through self-experiential prototyping, drawing upon theories put forth by game designers. The academic research part of Smith and Dean's (2009) model consists of new data obtained from models and autoethnographic research.

I used autoethnography as a self-reflective device (Creswell, 2002), which I applied to the creative process of prototyping via reflection. According to Creswell (2002) and Reed-Danahay (1997), autoethnographic research connects one's personal experience with the broader sociocultural context. Autoethnography is a form of prose and exploration of connective self-experience. According to Luitel (2009), personal and professional experiences form the basis of personal inquiry. In this research project, my autoethnography was the act of producing creative work and reflecting upon this process of creation via reflective journal entries (please see Table 6.1).

I conducted autoethnographic research to reflect on the creation of my XR opera versions. Autoethnography analyses one's personal/self-experience and culture. It is about reflecting upon one's experience and improving one's practice (Belbase, Luitel, & Taylor, 2008; Ellis & Bochner, 2000). I employed reflective autoethnography in the form of free journaling each time I worked on a new iteration of the XR opera to reflect upon the various prototyping methodologies developed, leading to the creation of the models and Table 6.1 later in this book. Table 6.1 is the autoethnographic journal entries. The models refer to the figures later on in this book.

1.7 Conclusion

I undertook this research project as a novel way of comparing self-experiential prototyping processes of XR opera creation. What was revealed in relation to the research questions was that by fusing digital creation, composition, and XR, I conducted narrative research by studying my subjective experience. Josselson (2010) states that the aim of narrative research is the exploration and conceptualisation of human experience, as one is meant to use textual forms in narrative research; I documented my creative process textually so that others may use it to learn how to create new operas for a digital future. My research was influenced by prior research in VR, AR, XR, and immersive theatre. In Chapter 2, I discuss this book's thematic context.

Notes

1 XR is not different from VR and AR. It is an umbrella term that encompasses both.
2 Extremely realistic in detail, including VR technologies.
3 Middleware is a hidden layer – software that allows communication and data management via translation between multiple distributed applications. 'A set of

prewritten software libraries and tools to help with the development of games. Common examples of middleware in games include 3D middleware like UDK and Unity, and audio middleware like Fmod and Wwise' (Sweet, 2015, p. 433). 'Audio middleware is a third-party tool set that sits between the game engine and the audio hardware. It provides common functionality that is needed on each project such as randomising pitch or volume, fading sounds in or out, and picking randomly a sound from a set of sounds' (Brown, n.d). The audio middleware used in early prototypes of the Oculus version of *Artemis* was FMOD Studio (see media example 26).

2 Thematic Context

In this chapter, I analyse immersive theatre as a new blurring of audience agency, explore digital opera, and examine the role of interactivity. I also analyse the composition and narrative storytelling aspects of the Gesamtkunstwerk[1] opera, as they are directly related to my methodology of digital Gesamtkunstwerk[2] opera creation.[3]

The audience's interactive participation leads to immersive experiences, which liberate the audience from previous conventions (Worthen, 2012). This is closely related to immersive theatre, in which the cognition of audience members is respected; they are not merely spectators. Interaction between the actors and audience members via touch, embrace, and dialogue creates an immersive experience (Beacham, 1994; Machon, 2017; Worthen, 2012). According to Biggin (2017), immersion can be considered 'both a sensation experienced by spectators and something crafted and facilitated by makers' (p. 24). Immersive theatre prioritises the audience experience, as do VR, AR, and XR experiences. Machon (2017) defines immersive theatre as a work that 'prioritises human contact' (p. xvi).

For audiences to be immersed in an architectural artwork or a Gesamtkunstwerk, there must be a connection between the performer and the spectator (Hann, 2012). Seminal scenographer Appia created a performance architecture model, envisioning an opera future in which visual and musical art forms support one another to form one work of digital unity[4] (Hann, 2012). Appia alluded to immersive digital opera (Sheil & Vear, 2012) as a form in which the spectator is a participant (Beacham, 1994). In Appia's vision of living art, audience members are immersed in the art form and actively participate in the narrative (Beacham, 1994). According to Hann (2012), digital opera (Sheil & Vear, 2012) and 'intermedial' architecture may be used to explore Appia's concept of living art. Further, according to Emmerson (1998), 'sound has the power to create its own visual response in humans – one which is sometimes not accounted for by visual artists – a sense of place, of aural landscape' (p. 139). These two views can be combined to increase interactivity by interweaving immersive technologies with music to enhance the aural landscape and produce a sense of place for the audience.

DOI: 10.4324/9781003642541-2

Conversely, the virtual as a 'representation' has been thoroughly explored by Ryan (2001), who states that 'the virtual takes the place of the real and becomes the hyper real' (p. 29). Ryan (2001) explored the hyperreality theory proposed by Baudrillard, who argued that representations of the outside world become a person's reality. Humans cannot differentiate between reality and simulations of reality (Ryan, 2001). Ryan also considered Pierre Lévy's work on representation, whose book *What is the virtual?* contradicts Baudrillard's claims (Murphie, 1997). Lévy's view on representation is that the virtual is not concurrent with illusions or fantastical elements and does not diverge from the real.

Furthermore, regarding interactivity, Benford and Giannachi (2011) refer to 'interaction' as performing with mixed realities by creating a performance framework using new technologies. In their view, the next generations of artists will create mixed-reality works that combine theatre, VR, and actors, and participants will perform using interactive media to create new user experiences. Combining narrative with interactivity has been proposed by scholars. According to Meadows (2003), a narrative is presented from the creators' perspective, which is the single most crucial aspect of storytelling. An interactive narrative 'is a narrative form that allows someone other than the author to affect, choose, or change the plot' (Meadows, 2003, p. 2) of a story or experience. Aronson (1999) asks, 'If advancements in dramaturgy can lead to developments in theatre architecture and technology, should not the reverse also be true?' (p. 189). Building on this, AR and VR technologies may develop new dramaturgy, just as Baroque opera was created by combining 'architecture, technology, and scenography' (Aronson, 2005, p. 191). The fusion of digital media and music creates a new form of performance art, and technological developments can lead to new developments in storytelling.

Further, Benford and Giannachi (2012) used ethnography to explore user experiences. Benford and Giannachi (2012) used artists' rationales and employed an iterative cycle to explore how the various activities of touring and interaction feed into one another as artist-led research. They aimed to create a concept and framework for studies in this novel field, to create a 'boundary object' at the crossroads of human–computer interaction, theatre, and performance studies. They also argued that mixed reality could incorporate various forms of interface design into a coherent new experience created by multiple mediums.

Following the theories put forth by Benford and Giannachi (2011), digital opera represents a new form of multisensory art; multisensory art is interactive. An example is Hotel Pro Forma's *Tomorrow, in a Year* (2009), produced in collaboration with the electro-band The Knife (Hann, 2012). This beautifully staged electro-opera breaks the rules of traditional opera to create a cohesive and highly innovative art form by combining dance, acting, architecture, and projections.

Studies have suggested that AR enhances social presence and increases learning through curiosity (Jung, tom Dieck, Lee, & Chung, 2016). AR has a long-lasting 'experiential impact' (Javornik, Rogers, Gander, & Moutinho, 2017), as it is perceived as entertaining, fun, and educational. According to Shankar, Kleijnen, Ramanathan, Rizley, Holland, and Morrissey (2016), AR, VR, and mixed reality are a way of delivering new content to consumers. Digital elements draw people into a story (Javornik, Rogers, Gander, & Moutinho, 2017). My research builds upon this concept of drawing people into the narrative using new technologies. According to Ryan (2001), immersion and interactivity are the two constituents of VR. To provide a compelling experience, VR should cohesively combine immersive elements and interactivity.

Pointing to multisensory experiences, there must be a bridge between aural and visual art forms. Expanding on this, Hann (2012) states that experiential aspects, such as smell, can be included in digital opera. The smell of cedar oil was incorporated into a multisensory opera pioneered by Appia in the Festspielhaus Hellerau. According to Hann, combining sensory aspects can be added to the architecture of the experience in the concert house, in which the sonic and experiential aspects become a meeting point with the architecture of the concert hall.

Multisensory work is, in essence, multimodal. Multimodal can be defined as 'having or involving several modes, modalities, or maxima' (Merriam-Webster, n.d.).

AR can enhance opera's multimodal experience. Marasco, Balbi, and Icolari (2018) highlighted the need for further research on multisensory AR opera.

Auslander considers live performances clichéd in their description, which he describes as 'magic' (Auslander, 1999, p. 2). Auslander argues that framing and describing a live experience is not helpful to the artists or the spectators, who are removed from the creation of the experience. This is important to my project, in which the spectator sees the world from a first-person perspective. Wurtzler (1992) explored the differences between live and recorded mediums as representations, placing the two in separate groups. Auslander (1999) challenged this traditional view by criticising the duality of these supposedly opposite concepts of live (real) and mediatised (artificial replication of the real) events. Auslander explored the 'ontology of live performance' and defined mediatised performance as 'performance that is circulated on television, as audio or video recordings, and in other forms based in technologies of reproduction' (p. 4). In my view, XR music productions are a new form of mediatised performance. Composing and creating for VR could indeed be a completely new medium. MAYA is a VR music experience that exists already, pushing the boundaries and blurring the roles of composer, producer, and user.

According to Wurtzler (1992), there are four pairs of opposites: live versus recorded, event versus representation, original versus copy, and spatial co-presence (live events) versus spatial absence (mediated televised events). Adorno (Cook, 1996) coined the term 'culture industry', which could refer to live performances being replaced with mediatised forms of mass-produced culture.

Bolter and Grusin (1996) argued that new modes of reproduction can use new technologies to revolutionise earlier forms. From these perspectives, we learn that a mediatised performance is a reproduced performance. This is relevant to my research, as the XR opera I created is a reproduction of the same musical score in different versions.

Van Elferen (2016) explored immersive game sound. Van Elferen (2016) states that game soundtracks enhance immersion in a computer game. Collins (2008) also notes that sound increases immersion in computer games, acting as a metaphor for the visual VR of a game. In my view, music is essential for increasing immersion and coherence in a game's visual and narrative journey by increasing the user's emotional engagement. Music makes the player connect to the game character and become the hero.

Female characters rarely survive the age of 20 in opera (McClary, 2011). It has been suggested that more narratives about female protagonists are needed in the opera genre (Clément, 1988). Narrative choices should include an autonomous female perspective, as a 'feminine perspective is foreign to the contingent cultural history of opera' (Klein, 2014, p. 77). Therefore, my opera focuses on the story of a strong female character, Artemis. It is an opera in which women's voices are honoured.

Other opera makers and scholars have argued for reimagining traditional operas in which women are positioned as the weaker sex (Blackwood, Lim, Polias, & Van Reyk, 2019; Clément, 1988; Klein, 2014; McClary, 2011; Smart, 1992). I deliberately crafted a narrative reflecting contemporary notions of gender, as opposed to canonical operatic narrative tropes in which female characters are depicted as objects to be conquered by male characters. Artemis aims to be part of a new era of opera in which women do not need to die as a dramaturgical element. Artemis aims to create a new female-centric narrative that supports, rather than destroys, a strong female character (Botsman, 2020).

2.1 Conclusion

In conclusion, what was revealed was that immersive theatre prioritises the audience experience, as do VR, AR, and XR experiences. Concurrently, for audiences to be part of an architectural artwork or a Gesamtkunstwerk, there must be a connection between the performer and the spectator. Further, scholars state that AR work that includes entertainment, fun, and educational elements increases learning through curiosity. Scholars say that sound is necessary for successful experiences. In Chapter 3, I delve deeper into relevant creative works and opera content and discuss how they relate to my research.

Notes

1 Wagnerian opera fuses stage design, myth, dramatic narratives, and singing to create cohesive immersive phenomena in a 'total work' – a 'Gesamtkunstwerk' in German (Ortiz-de-Urbina, 2020).
2 See Macpherson (2012).
3 A complete history of opera is beyond the scope of this thesis. For an entire history, see Abbate and Parker (2012); Grout, Grout, and Williams (2003); Parker (2001).
4 Unity does not refer to the software in this instance.

3 Review of Relevant Artworks

This chapter presents an integrated discussion of relevant artworks. It also explores non-traditional techniques of opera creation, which are relevant to the exploration of my research questions.

In this chapter, I will argue that opera companies have begun incorporating AR and VR experiences into their seasons to attract a diverse audience and younger viewers. To reveal the scope of XR experimentation in opera, I explore XR works that the Bayerische Staatsoper, Opera Australia, the Welsh National Opera Company, and re:Naissance have included in their programs. I also discuss Punchdrunk's *Sleep No More* (2003), *The Firebird Ball* (2005), and *Faust* (2006), all directed by Felix Barrett; Dot Dot Dot's *SOMNAI: Lucid dreaming* (2017), with creative technology direction by Carl Guyenette; Thatgamecompany's *Journey* (2012); and Nyamyam's *Astrologaster* (2019).

Pioneering opera productions have embraced AR and VR elements to breathe new life into the opera gesnre and increase audience engagement. For example, MagicFace is an AR app that engages younger audiences by projecting the make-up styles of the lead characters from Philip Glass' opera *Akhnaten* (1995), Akhnaten and Nefertiti, onto one's face (Javornik, Rogers, Gander, & Moutinho, 2017). VR animation began to take off with the Welsh National Opera's *Magic Butterfly VR* (2017), VR director Greg Furber. VR 360° productions emerged with the Bayerische Staatsoper's *V-Aria* (2018), directed by Daniel Moshel, and Teatro Real's *Porgy and Bess 360* (2015), directed by Christine Crouse.

Pioneering experiments using VR for stage design began in 2004 (Reaney, Unruh, & Hudson-Mairet, 2004). A digitally augmented opera production, *The Magic Flute VR*, was based on a virtual stage created with interactive 3D graphics controlled by a technician and the performers (Kajastila & Takala, 2008). *The Magic Flute VR* employed real-time computer graphics, using multiple manually moved audio-reactive projection screens and Computergenerated Imagery (CGI) characters on digital projection screens. As this production was entirely digital, it was portable and did not require a physical set. In conjunction with PureData and GEM software, Wii remote controls allowed the performers to change the 3D graphics whilst performing. The 3D

DOI: 10.4324/9781003642541-3

graphics reflected the characters' thoughts. The staging became a real-time interactive element rather than a stationary backdrop for the performance. The performers also controlled a 5.1 surround sound system to create a spinning soundscape, matching a spinning roulette visual operated by hand gestures and the pitch and roll functions of the Wii remote controls. Thus, technology enabled real-time interplay between visual effects, narrative, and music. However, having to control stage elements whilst singing added to the stress experienced by the performers, who were worried they might make a mistake; for this reason, a backstage technician was also employed to control the graphics (Kajastila & Takala, 2008).

The Magic Flute VR was a precursor to VR and AR opera. With VR and AR mediums, performers do not need to worry about controlling technology whilst performing, as the VR and AR content is developed prior to the performance (Kajastila & Takala, 2008).

Pioneers in XR and opera in the UK are Opera Beyond, who have a VR production ecosystem model for innovative productions in XR (Kennedy & Atkinson, 2018). The Opera of the Future group at MIT Media Lab (see Jessop, Torpey, & Bloomberg, 2011) have also done some really interesting innovative work relating to interaction design and performance productions.

A Gesamtkunstwerk is a total work combining multiple art forms, including mythology, to create one cohesive work. Whilst early operas of the seventeenth and eighteenth centuries drew upon mythology (Espinosa, 2007), Richard Wagner created the Gesamtkunstwerk in the nineteenth century by linking myth, narrative, and music in his operas (Ortiz-de-Urbina, 2020). The importance of synthesising multiple art forms can be likened to the argument that, according to Ryan (2001), immersion and interactivity create total art, synthesising the mind and body and providing a cohesive participant experience. Synthesising multiple art forms occurs in XR experiences through onboarding objects and activities, virtual environments, and potentially built physical sets.

The Gesamtkunstwerk was a concept emerging out of Richard Wagner's multimodal opera experience creation; Wagner built an entire theatre in Bayreuth Festival Theatre to increase immersion in the opera production for audience members (Spotts, 1994). Wagner believed it was artificial to use different song forms as it removed immersion; thus, the Gesamtkunstwerk operas were through-composed (Deathridge, 1974); this is important as I used the through-composed technique for *Artemis*. The concept of onboarding, which is discussed in this chapter, is a modern version of Wagner's Bayreuth theatre. The onboarding objects in *Sleep No More* are a modern equivalent of the multimodal Bayreuth theatre. Immersive theatre's transferability to opera is highlighted in this chapter, with VR onboarding activities being the modern, cost-effective version of the Bayreuth theatre immersion. There is a connection between the Gesamtkunstwerk and ideas of immersion and presence built on onboarding activities and objects in XR experiences; this has been theorised by Striner, Halpin, Röggla, and César Garcia (2021) who stated, 'Democratising opera consists of creating an intuitive technology onboarding process' (p. 315).

In immersive theatre, onboarding objects and activities integrate the audience into the experience. For example, in *Sleep No More*, the onboarding object is a white mask worn by audience members, whilst in *SOMNAI: Lucid dreaming*, the front-of-house staff checks in the audience members, and their faces are scanned. Onboarding refers to getting people into the technology and the XR experience (Wilkinson & Appanah, 2020) and is related to the narrative. It deviates from the tradition of cinema, in which there is a clear distinction between the content creator and the content consumer (Wilkinson & Appanah, 2020). Offboarding refers to seamlessly getting people out of the experience, out of the technology, and back into the physical world. Onboarding and offboarding give space to the individual, as each participant is different; some are extroverts and want to participate in the narrative (Wilkinson & Appanah, 2020), whereas others can act as passive observers and traditional spectators. Onboarding draws on a concept from writing: one does not start in a fantastic world; a portal transports one to the fantastic world (Wilkinson & Appannah, 2020). For example, in *The Lion, The Witch and the Wardrobe* by Lewis (1950), the wardrobe is the vehicle for transitioning to the fantastic world (Wilkinson & Appannah, 2020).

Seminal immersive theatre productions have been created by Punchdrunk, founded by University of Exeter alumni in 2000. The company has created immersive theatre works that have emotional impact (Worthen, 2012). The three Punchdrunk productions explored in this review of relevant artworks use new ways of engaging audiences. Punchdrunk differs from other theatre companies in using time-looped sequences coordinated with music instead of traditional theatre scenes (Eglinton, 2010). Its creative process includes four stages. First, in the research and planning stages, the artistic directors Felix Barrett and Maxine Doyle reimagine a classical work. Second, rehearsals take place in a studio. Third, the rehearsals are transferred to a site-specific venue.[1] Finally, the production is fine-tuned to create a site-specific work for a live audience (Eglinton, 2010). This process is relevant to my creative process, including four stages. In the first stage, I conducted research and planning. In the second stage, I held rehearsals. I transferred the *Artemis* AR opera to a site-specific venue in the third stage. In the fourth stage, I fine-tuned the performance for a live audience by cohesively putting up AR posters in the Nickson Room performance venue.

Punchdrunk typically draws on classical texts. *Sleep No More* (Barrett & Doyle, 2003) was its first production to remove all dialogue. This work recreated *Macbeth* (Shakespeare, 1611). Punchdrunk used masks to create an onboarding experience to heighten immersion and interaction.[2] The masks provided anonymity and encouraged the audience members to embark on an adventure. Worthen (2012) likened this activity to being assigned a seat in an auditorium. The live theatre version of *Sleep No More* is relevant to my research, as it is relevant to the current *Artemis* work of having users roam the performance space in a free-form way and, in *Artemis XR*, users interact with the AR material rather than the actors as is the case in Punchdrunk's works. In future *Artemis* XR performances, I will use physical onboarding objects to reiterate textual libretto elements tactilely. To create a multisensory experience, I will use scent by spraying rose water. In the current YouTube VR 360° versions, virtual elements are linked to the libretto. For example, the virtual stars are linked to the stars in the 'Licht und Liebe' spring duet libretto.

Punchdrunk's six-week immersive theatre production *The Firebird Ball* (Barrett & Doyle, 2005) was a site-specific work in a disused factory warehouse in London that drew upon *Romeo and Juliet* (Shakespeare, 2009) combined with the composer Stravinsky's *The Firebird* (Eglinton, 2010). The production was sold out and earned critical acclaim (Eglinton, 2010, p. 48). It included a live band and 14 performers and used architectural lighting, audio, and installation work accompanied by coordinated performances (Eglinton, 2010) in multiple rooms. In one room was a white forest with firebirds dancing among feather-filled trees. The character Tybalt contorted himself at a purple-lit entrance, and audience members had to weave their way under the contortionist. In another dark room filled with the scent of incense, a priest was murmuring. In another room, Romeo and Tybalt had a choreographed roving duel among audience members (Eglinton, 2010). As in *Sleep No More*, the audience members wore masks as an immersion onboarding activity, and each member was encouraged to move through the space individually. Punchdrunk's works are related to my project, as I encouraged each audience member to walk around the virtual and augmented space during the *Artemis* XR performances and exhibitions. Moreover, Punchdrunk's productions are dissimilar to my project, as the only text in *Artemis* is the libretto; that is why *Artemis* is similar to traditional opera, in which the only text is usually the libretto.

Punchdrunk's *Faust* (Barrett & Doyle, 2006), staged in a multistorey warehouse in London (Eglinton, 2010), expanded Goethe's (1832) *Faust* to create a mixed-methods production. Multisensory tactile, kinaesthetic, and physical elements converged to create an embodied experience (Eglinton, 2010). As in *Sleep No More*, the spectators were given masks to create a feeling of role-playing (Eglinton, 2010). For some, the masks acted as cloaking devices, enabling them to blend into the surroundings, whereas for others, they were an open invitation to perform (Eglinton, 2010). Thus, the masks created the experience of an interior world (Worthen, 2012). *Faust* is related to my work as it is also a mixed-methods production in which audience members roam around the performance venue.

SOMNAI: Lucid dreaming (2017), staged in London, is a mixed-reality production combining immersive theatre strategies with VR. SOMNAI was another production that used onboarding activities. It combined VR and escape rooms, with audience members wearing VR headsets and touching objects and sets whilst immersed in a horror escape room experience (Haake, 2019). The show was created by the VR theatre company Ellipsis Entertainment, Dot Dot Dot, and Target3D. Physical sets based on tactile elements were crucial to the virtual experience. The specialist team Target3D created the virtual environment using Unity3D. Another specialised team generated aromas to evoke different emotions. The audience members made choices that determined the show's narrative.

Thus, each participant's experience was unique (Wilkinson & Appannah, 2020). As part of the experience, the participants walked down Old Street in East London and encountered a discreet dark door, which acted as the portal to the world they were about to enter. The world was dark, and audio was used to change the participants' perceptions coming from a busy London street. In the first onboarding step, the front-of-house staff spoke in the tone and language of the show, and audience members spent 15 minutes onboarding whilst handing over their coats. In the second step, the audience members' faces were scanned. A sign on the wall said that the participants' brains were being 'checked in'. The participants encountered the *SOMNAI: Lucid dreaming* AI character 15 minutes later but were already immersed in the experience through the onboarding activities and audio. Through onboarding, the participants became 'patients' and were given patient IDs after their faces were scanned. According to one of the *SOMNAI: Lucid dreaming* creators, Myra Appannah (Wilkinson & Appanah, 2020), there may have been points that escaped the participants' attention, such as technical elements used to transition them in and out of the VR headsets and, thus, between the physical and virtual worlds, and these formerly awkward and clunky moments were turned around by the creators as narrative moments through onboarding.

In conclusion, immersive theatre relies on audience members' participation. Audience members are not merely spectators but 'experiencers' of the production and characters around them (Worthen, 2012). Immersive experiences evoke different emotions; each participant journeys through sound, acting, and sets (Eglinton, 2010; Worthen, 2012).

3.1   Interactive Music and Games

I drew inspiration from video games; I did this by playing various games. Two games that stood out for me in their design and sound implementation were *Journey* (Thatgamecompany, 2012) and *Astrologaster* (Nyamnyam, 2019).

The video game *Journey* (Thatgamecompany, 2012) was composed by Austin Wintory and released by Thatgamecompany in 2012. There is no dialogue in the game. The music seamlessly unfolds in real time, and the sound effects and foley are optimally implemented. In level 1, a staggered entry and branching composition are employed, a drone begins, and a harp plays arpeggiated notes. A violin motif enters, and the harp crescendos, with a female voice (Elizabeth Scott) singing in an unspecified Nordic language. The violin re-enters, and a beat enters to increase the tension. Music is used as a narrative device. The sound effects of running in orange dunes and the wind sound effects are the only elements in the immersive sound environment until the player reaches the top of a dune. When the player reaches the top of the dune, the music changes to a solo cello playing an evocative melody accompanied by plucked zither strings and a flute. A synth pad adds ambient accompaniment under the solo cello melody. A chime is used as an interactive UI sound when the user starts the game. At the beginning of the game, standing on the dune, the player hears the rustling of scarf fabric and reads the word 'Journey'.

The gameplay requires the player to collect pieces of fabric to lengthen their scarf and add textures and patterns. The player uses the up UI button to jump and the left-hand button to collect fabric, which lights up when collected. The pieces of fabric have bird sound effects, and fabric flapping sounds are mapped to the fabric scraps whilst they fly around. The player must jump to collect the pieces of fabric and dance with them whilst collecting them. Throughout the game, when the player jumps and collects the flying fabric scraps, the UI sounds change depending on whether the player activates totem poles to open gates to the next level or lengthens the scarf.

Tibetan bells and dissonant electronic sounds accompany level 2. In this level, the player must collect the fabric by jumping and then activate each large piece of cloth to build a cloth bridge to reach a waterfall, the level portal. A beat is activated when the player runs across the cloth bridge. Once the player reaches the level portal, they sit down, and a mother figure appears in front of a magical mountain.

Level 3 has pink dunes. The more fabric the player collects, the more details appear on the ancient buildings and ruins. The player creates manta ray kites, which lead the way. These manta ray kites have dolphin and whale sonar sound effects. There is an amphitheatre where the player collects another lengthening scarf token that glows white. A double bass played pizzicato accompanies the journey. There is a desolate windblown zone with a sandstorm, which is disorientating. It is difficult to pass level 3, as the music is dissonant and evokes emotions of unease. Thus, *Journey* (Thatgamecompany, 2012) is interactive; it is a seminal video game that successfully combines sound design and composition to create an art aesthetic. The music interactivity and realistic sound design have made it essential to the music and gaming communities. It exemplifies creating effective interactive musical–art experiences for handheld devices. *Journey* is relevant to my Unity3D version of *Artemis*, in which I used interactive sound design and music.

Compared to the open-world non-linear game *Journey*, the video game *Astrologaster* (Nyamnyam, 2019) is a narrative game released by Nyamnyam in 2019. It has a pop-up picture book design aesthetic, featuring harpsichord, operatic, and choral arrangements in its score. There are multiple narrative environments, namely four main game scenes:

1. There is a consultation room akin to a theatre stage where the main game character Simon Foreman, who lives during the black plague, interviews his patients.
2. There is an astrology tile screen on which the player reads the stars. Interactive UI sounds are activated when the player chooses a tile during a reading. The 'Choose one zodiac to diagnose the condition' screen is accompanied by a meditative synth pad that loops when the player chooses an astrology card as a specific cure, a soprano sings 'ah', and a chime sounds on top of the meditative synth.
3. There is an SATB choral theme for each game character.
4. There is a screen where an olden-day news crier announces the news.

Astrologaster is related to my research, as I created a video game-like experience with electro-opera scoring by combining synth pads, a mezzo-soprano singer, a tenor singer, and traditional Western notation similar to the sound palette heard in *Astrologaster* (AIR-EDEL MUSIC, 2019). Moreover, *Astrologaster* (Nyamnyam, 2019) is historical fiction, as it draws upon and represents a historical time, namely the narrative of the black plague. *Artemis* is based on Greek mythology and draws on mythological events, whereas Astologaster (Nyamnyam, 2019) draws on historical events. The sound worlds of *Journey* and *Astrologaster* differ in timbres and sound implementation, and inspired the sound world of *Artemis*.

Whilst *Journey* is a free-roaming game similar to the Oculus VR version of *Artemis*, *Astrologaster* is a pre-ordered game similar to the recorded YouTube VR version of *Artemis*.

3.2 XR and Opera

The Bayerische Staatsoper, Opera Australia, and the Welsh National Opera have begun integrating VR and AR elements into their opera productions and concert programs. *V-Aria – Opera in VR and 360°* (Moshel, 2018) is a three-minute 360° VR experience. The participant sits in a red velvet chair wearing a VR headset and is teleported through the opera house to meet the musicians, dancers, and singers. The participant can hear the music and see the sets and halls behind the scenes. The opera singers then perform on stage, followed by 2,000 audience members applauding. Another 360° VR production is Teatro Real's *360VR Porgy and Bess* (director unknown, 2015), a traditional opera staging of composer Gershwin's *Porgy and Bess*. The production is dissimilar to *V-Aria – Opera in VR and 360°*, as *360VR Porgy and Bess* uses floating text boxes to indicate the characters during the performance. The Royal Opera House created the interactive VR experience *Join the Royal*

Opera Chorus in 360° (Royal Opera House, 2016). According to the creators, the experience was like singing as a chorus member of the *Nabucco* opera composed by Verdi in a first-person VR experience (Royal Opera House, 2016). The creators also stated that this work's impact on opera was that anyone could live like an opera performer, thus potentially inspiring prospective performers (Royal Opera House, 2016).

These three 360° VR films were considered by their creators to offer a new way of disseminating opera to remote audiences.

Another company that released its first iteration of a VR opera in 2017 in collaboration with REWIND VR was The Welsh National Opera Company. The opera, titled *The Magic Butterfly VR Experience (*Eiddior, 2017; Welsh National Opera, 2022), was a highly successful animated production based on *Madame Butterfly* by the composer Puccini, and *The Magic Flute*, by the composer Mozart that toured in a shipping container throughout the UK, as well as in Hong Kong, Copenhagen, and Dubai, along with multiple Google Daydream View VR headsets and headphones (Welsh National Opera, 2022). The Welsh National Opera's innovative use of VR, an amalgamation of music, technology, and art, and the heroine Cio Cio San performing 'One Fine Day' and 'How Soft, How Strong Your Magic Sound' reached new audiences and was positively received, with 12,000 people attending the production during the tour (Welsh National Opera, 2022). The VR animation was produced using a motion capture suit with mesh attached to imitate the movement of a kimono's sleeves. Whilst the soprano Karah Son sang an aria, her movements were mapped, and the captured data were then used to create an avatar (Haptical, 2017). The site-specific aspect of the production, the use of new motion capture technologies to create an avatar singing in a virtual environment, and the use of animal assets contributed to successfully reimagining two works.

OrpheusVR (Reallusion, 2022) reimagines composer Monteverdi's *L'Orfeo* as a VR opera (Renaissance Opera, 2021). Like *The Magic Butterfly VR Experience*, *OrpheusVR* (Reallusion, 2022) uses motion capture technology to create a choose-your-own-adventure VR opera prototype. The production *Eight* (Van der Aa, 2018) uses motion capture and VR alongside a classical score. *Eight* transports the audience through multiple environments, whilst the audience never leaves a small room. VR technologies are interwoven with Western classical music (Michel Van der Aa, 2019). These productions successfully use video game engines and film technologies to create new immersive opera experiences.

Various attempts have been made to combine AR technologies with traditional opera productions. An example is the MagicFace AR application. The project involved developing the app and the interface and working with the English National Opera. The app was used with composer Philip Glass's opera *Akhnaten*. The research project consisted of two studies. The MagicMirror developers recruited two groups of users to test the app. The first group consisted of children, and the second included opera performers (Javornik

Rogers, Gander, & Moutinho, 2017). These groups helped the developers identify features they could add to the app, collect considerable data, and observe how people interacted with this new technology (Javornik, Rogers, Gander, & Moutinho, 2017).

In study 1, users augmented the look of Pharaoh Akhnaten or Queen Nefertiti, the main characters in the opera *Akhnaten* (Javornik, Rogers, Gander, & Moutinho, 2017). To make the *Akhnaten* experience engaging, the app ran on an iPad Pro in a dressing room disguised as a mirror in the English National Opera Coliseum opera house (Javornik, Rogers, Gander, & Moutinho, 2017). The use of technology blended into the traditional world of opera houses and extended the experience whilst remaining true to the traditional opera format. The school-aged participants had not engaged with opera before the study. The app engaged them by showing them what goes on behind the scenes of an opera production, such as hair styling and make-up (Javornik, Rogers, Gander, & Moutinho, 2017). The participants in the second group were opera experts; therefore, the ways in which they interacted with the app were different (Javornik, Rogers, Gander, & Moutinho, 2017). They used the technology to replicate the physical make-up they usually wore during their performances.

In study 2, the MagicFace app ran on an iPad Pro embedded in a picture frame and displayed in the Petrie Museum of Egyptian Archaeology exhibit *Akhnaten*; people interacted with it by walking up to the iPad Pro picture frame, by chance and having AR filters applied to their faces. The exhibition visitors were not informed of the iPad's presence, whereas in the opera house, visitors were explicitly informed. The significance of this was that the study varied due to the transparency of the AR medium; in the exhibit, users stumbled upon the AR filter by chance, whereas in the opera house, they were fully aware of the AR filter (Javornik, Rogers, Gander, & Moutinho, 2017).

These studies demonstrated how new technologies can be used to engage new audiences. The MagicFace project is important because it engages users in a world where they can try on make-up and get a sense of what it feels like to be an opera singer in costume (Javornik, Rogers, Gander, & Moutinho, 2017).

AR has also been used in concert programs. An example is The Royal Swedish Opera Augmented Reality (Royal Swedish Opera, 2020). When the user turns the page, the classical music of each production seems to play from the page, and the 3D animation jumps out at the user in a magical fashion. The AR additions to the 2D catalogue include the opera theatre, a growing tree, a performer's skeleton and organs, a flying cape, and fog. Sets come to life in 3D, and ballerinas emerge from the catalogue. Dancing animations emerge and float in mid-air. Another example of an AR concert program is Opera Australia Augmented Reality (Opera Australia, 2010), created by EXPLOREENGAGE. Users hold the program up to a laptop camera to view the augmented elements, and 3D text emerges from the program, such as 'EXPERIENCE A NIGHT AT THE OPERA'. For the *Pearl Fishers*, by composer Bizet, the set comes alive in 3D. These AR technologies thus turn 2D programs into immersive artefacts.

Tapestry Opera, a company spearheaded by Debi Wong, created the augmented opera TAP: EX. The main character, Eurydice, wears a VR headset whilst singing. TAP: EX was warmly received by audiences and won critical acclaim.

Another AR opera is *Maya* (Nitschke, 2018), which claims to be the first AR opera experience. It was staged in 2017 in an old heating plant in Munich-Aubing and was a commercial success (Nitschke, 2018). The performers walked on raised platforms through the audience members. Using an AR app on their smartphones, the audience members looked at a future civilisation; the main character, Maya (Martina Koppelstetter), is on a mission to save cyberspace, herself, and humanity. *Maya* made an impact by having audience members use smartphones effectively in an AR performance. According to Nitschke, integrating new technologies into productions where audience members do not switch off their phones is necessary (Roesner, 2018).

Opera Queensland's AR Experience is an AR app developed with Google for Siggraph 2020; it is a reimagined version of *The Magic Flute* by the composer Mozart; the work is experienced on a smartphone and comes alive in the user's living room. This Opera Queensland prototype was based on the novel use of animated characters.

The impact of AR on the evolution of opera is the inclusion and integration of smartphones and novel technologies to create new experiences. The impact of VR is the use of site-specific works rather than traditional opera houses, in which audience members are seated spectators and must turn off their phones (Nitschke, 2018). Multiple non-traditional opera works which used novel techniques have been composed by Mathis Nitschke (Roesner, 2018), who used techniques that are becoming popular in music festivals, such as Tête à Tête, the Munich Biennale, and the Prototype Festival in New York. These AR and VR techniques extended compositional practices and traditional opera to create site-specific performances for younger audiences. Nitschke creates multidisciplinary art by renegotiating the traditional aspects of theatre and spectatorship (Roesner, 2018). His goal is to convey the inclusive nature of opera (Roesner, 2018). As in Punchdrunk's immersive theatre works, in *Maya* (Nitschke, 2018), audience members are not mere observers but part of the performance. The audience members use a smartphone app that overlays AR content onto the heating plant's walls. The AR content adds a layer before the opera starts that adds to the site-specific element of the experience. The audience members see artefacts that provide hints about what happened and walk around to explore what is happening. The opera then starts, and audience members can look inside the heating plant oven using their smartphones as X-ray devices. They see creatures that 'once lived' and tell the story of what happened in this site-specific venue. The AR app creates the feeling of being present in the old heating plant through text and images of old equipment overlayed onto the wall ruins that reveal parts of the story. The audience members also interact with each other, creating a social immersion experience, which is part of the concept. The AR creatures try to use the audience members' smartphones to speak to Maya. Thus, the sound is used from each user's phone, creating a spatial experience as the phones make noise and their flashlights are turned on. The users are asked to point their flashlights to light up Maya and follow her around. Thus, the users become part of the performance (Nitschke, 2018a, 2018b). *Maya* is like a puzzle game in which the audience members unveil the story using AR elements (Roesner, 2018). The exploratory element of *Maya* is similar to the UQ BLOOM Festival performance of *Artemis*, in which audience members explored the Nickson Room to find and scan 11 AR art overlays.

Technology can be used to enhance site-specific performances through smartphones. Opera creators aim to use technology in novel ways to immerse audiences in XR worlds. Site-specific works such as *Maya* (Nitschke, 2018) are the forerunners of new opera.

Another work which employed AR in a novel fashion was *A Vixen's Tale* (Welsh National Opera, 2019; Jaehnig, 2019), a tunnel book AR reimagining of *The Cunning Little Vixen* by the composer Janáček. The production aimed to engage younger audiences (Welsh National Opera, n.d.). It used physical sets and AR illustrations to create an immersive experience for young operagoers.

Another example of a work that employed new technology was Lucas, Cornish, and Margolis's (2012) case study, which used Second Life mixed-reality technologies to create virtual worlds. The project created a live digital staging of *The Marriage of Figaro* by the composer Mozart in Second Life. Lucas, Cornish, and Margolis (2012) stated that conditioning involves arriving at the physical venue early, talking to other attendees, dancing, or drinking before the performance. This conditioning can be considered a form of onboarding. In *OperaBis*, avatars were teleported to the front of the building and walked down virtual corridors and through a virtual door to the performance venue. This conditioning, or onboarding, the activity of finding the concert hall, replicated the physical experience of attending a concert. In Second Life, attendees can arrive late at the concert, as the virtual doors are always open (Lucas, Cornish, & Margolis, 2012).

All the works discussed above used technology in innovative new ways; they immersed the audience through 360° experiences, AR elements, and productions successfully used video game engines and film technologies to create new immersive opera experiences.

3.3 Non-linear Storytelling

The concept of non-linearity is essential to my project, as the proximity to various objects determines the order of sound playback in the Oculus Quest version of *Artemis*. Linear works are predetermined experiences, whereas non-linear works change through interaction with the medium (Spaniol, Klamma, Sharda, & Jarke, 2006). According to Spaniol, Klamma, Sharda, and Jarke (2006), 'A non-linear story may have different endings depending on the user interactions taking place during story consumption. Therefore, during the story creation process, there is not just a single path through the story, but many alternative paths' (Spaniol, Klamma, Sharda, & Jarke, 2006, p. 252).

Non-linear films also employ visual themes; an example of this is the visual theme of hair colour used in the film *Eternal Sunshine of the Spotless Mind* (Gondry, 2004). Two lovers, Clementine and Joel, break up and decide to erase their minds of the memories from their relationship so that they do not suffer after their breakup. Clementine has tangerine-dyed hair in memories preceding her and Joel's mind erasure procedures. Hair colour differentiates the past from the present, and Clementine's blue hair defines the present (after mind erasure); the scenes jump between the past and present, and her hair shows the time.

Further examples of films using parallel storyline techniques are *Run Lola Run* (Tykwer, 1998) and *Sliding Doors* (Howitt, 1998), in which the main characters' choices impact the narrative, and the viewer sees all alternate narratives. Amnesia is a non-linear device used in *Memento* (Nolan, 2000) and *Eternal Sunshine of the Spotless Mind* (Gondry, 2004) to fragment storylines into non-linear narratives. An example is *(500) Days of Summer* (Marc Webb, 2009), which uses flashbacks in a non-linear order to tell the story. Typewriter font spells out the day and goes back and forth in time. The film begins with montages of childhood footage of the two main characters, Tom and Summer, shown on each side of the screen. Such non-linear narratives create a more human memory-like experience.

Non-linear narratives structured as flashbacks or montages create a sense of living someone's life through their eyes. I implemented a similar narrative technique in *Artemis*, in which the music changes depending on the storyline that the user chooses in the Oculus Quest VR experience.

In non-linear novels, authors have used recurring motifs, such as buzzing bees jumping from the present to flashbacks in *The Beekeeper's Daughter* (Montefiore, 2005), and the date and location jumping between decades at the beginning of each chapter to create non-linearity. In *The Paris Seamstress* (Lester, 2018), letters telling the personal experiences of the different characters are used to link past and present storylines. Another device used in non-linear writing is the convergence of multiple stories. Examples are *Station Eleven* (St. John Mandel, 2014) and *All the Light We Cannot See* (Doerr, 2014), in which each character's journey is independent, and their journeys converge at the end.

Another non-linear device is time travel, used in *The Time Traveller's Wife* (Niffenegger, 2004), which occurs because the main character, Henry is genetically 'chrono-impaired'. Mary Hoffman also uses the non-linear time travel device in the *Stravaganza* series (Hoffman, 2008a, 2008b, 2010, 2012a,

2012b), which, in this case, is achieved with talismans. Each talisman is from an ancient Italian city, to which the main character is teleported upon discovering it hidden in modern-day London. Like *The Beekeeper's Daughter* (Montefiore, 2005), *All the Light We Cannot See* (Doerr, 2014), and *The Paris Seamstress* (Lester, 2018), *The Time Traveller's Wife* (Niffenegger, 2004) uses dates to denote time.

Like *The Time Traveller's Wife* (Niffenegger, 2004), the non-linear puzzle game Braid (Number None, 2009) utilises time travel. The aim is to find and collect all the puzzle pieces and rescue a princess. The player does not lose points when falling into the abyss below. Instead, the player can go back in time by pressing the space bar and redoing the action, such as climbing up a lattice. If the player falls onto a fire pit, a sound is activated, and a Shift key icon appears, which the player must press. Holding the Shift key turns back time and rotates the clouds and sun. The player can then retry the failed action. The linking of themes through the door portals is present throughout this non-linear game, creating a cohesive thread between the worlds. Braid's beautiful design consists of watercolour-like visuals of moving green and blue clouds and a rotating golden sun. Art-based outlines of the number of puzzle pieces the player can collect are shown. Lovely swaying iridescent green grasses dappled with sunlight and clumps of orange flowers are present at this game level. Once the player reaches a staircase with three steps, the text 'SPACE BAR' is engraved on the top step to indicate how the player can jump, and the music becomes staccato and fast; the steps' visuals relate to the music's staccato elements. Braid demonstrates how non-linear experiences are absorbed through life experiences; puzzle games are a genre of games in which players learn how to play the game as it progresses. Time is flexible, and the non-linear elements allow the player to choose where to go and which door to go through.

3.4 Conclusion

This chapter reviewed relevant artworks that influenced the creation of *Artemis*. What was revealed in relation to the second part of research question 1 – 'How can self-experiential prototyping methodologies be used to create new opera experiences?' – regarding creating new opera experiences was that immersive theatre devices can be used to make spectators part of the performance (Eglinton, 2010; Worthen, 2012). Innovative techniques and smartphone AR apps can enhance an opera's narrative, lighting, and staging (Nitschke, 2018). Non-linear devices such as visual themes, parallel storylines, flashbacks, montages, and amnesia have been employed in non-linear films. Novels used dates and time or time travel as non-linear devices. Video games use time travel to create non-linear game experiences. These non-linear devices aid in storytelling and immersion as they recreate the human experience, which is non-linear.

In Chapter 4, I outline how opera was inspired by Greek mythology. I explore various archetypes and interpretations of the Greek goddess Artemis throughout history.

Notes

1 A site-specific performance is a custom work developed for a public or new performance space.
2 An onboarding experience entails being drawn into the world of a performance via an object or performer.

4 Voicing Artemis

In this chapter, the two main points of focus are (1) Feminist opera and (2) Archetypes. I present a brief history of how opera was influenced by Greek mythology. I explore various representations and interpretations of the Greek goddess Artemis through the ages. To this end, I review the literature on the psychological archetypes of Artemis and her representations in sculptures and poetry. I then link Artemis' representations to the themes I used in my opera, explain my choices in the libretto development, and discuss how these choices are related to the mythological stories of the Greek goddesses Artemis and Gaia and the Greek god Orion. I also analyse the positioning of female characters in traditional opera.

Early operatic narratives were built on Greek myths (Klein, 2014). Greek mythology has inspired opera works due to the convergence of austerity and drama to create an engaging art form (Littlejohn, 1992). The Florentine Camerata created the earliest form of opera in the late sixteenth and early seventeenth centuries (Fawcett-Lothson, 2009). The Florentine Camerata was an intellectual collective inspired by Greek mythology, experimenting with reviving ancient Greek theatre. Its members included philosophers and thinkers who aimed to eliminate excessive musical ornamentation and highlighted the need for beautiful singing that expressed emotions without extravagant embellishments, which led to the creation of the aria form (Fawcett-Lothson, 2009).

Many operas based on Greek myths employ narratives with a male protagonist and a weak female character. The female character usually dies at the hands of the male protagonist (Clément, 1988). One such opera is Apollo & Daphne (Handel, 1710), in which Daphne dies by transforming herself into a laurel tree as Apollo tries to rape her. Another opera is Orpheus & Eurydice (Gluck, 1762), in which Eurydice dies as Orpheus looks at her whilst they travel from the underworld; the condition in Hades was that Orpheus was not allowed to look at her. However, Orpheus looks at her, and then Eurydice must die again; she is only brought back to life as a reward for Orpheus' continued love.

In art, Artemis is depicted as a huntress accompanied by a stag or a dog; this can be seen in various statues housed in the Louvre Museum, The

DOI: 10.4324/9781003642541-4

Voicing Artemis 29

Figure 4.1 Artemis with a Stag. Statue housed in the Louvre Museum. First or second century AD. Copy of a lost Greek bronze by Leochares, circa 325BC. Image by rjhuttondfw. Creative Commons – Attribution 2.0 Generic – CC BY 2.0. No changes made. [https://www.flickr.com/photos/rjhuttondfw/10678561295/in/photolist-2mBq3ZA-5hWYJJ-hgCqeM-8jVwdb-a9V7dq-3aY25-nZELcw].

Metropolitan Museum of Art, and the Vatican Museum. Various representations of Artemis in sources, such as poems, vases, and statues, depict Artemis with a hunting tunic, a quiver, a bow, and the moon. Figures 4.1–4.3 highlight different aspects of Artemis. In Figure 4.1, Artemis is represented as the goddess of hunting who protects nature, symbolised by her hand on the stag's

Figure 4.2 Limestone statue of the goddess Artemis housed at the MET. MET public domain image.

head, whilst embodying the psychological archetype of the huntress by placing her right hand on the arrows as if she is about to pull one out of her quiver. Her face is stoic, and the stag is fused to her side as if it is an extension of her persona. Artemis is wearing an almost masculine hunting tunic that reaches her knees instead of the traditional women's tunic reaching the ground.

Figure 4.2 shows the close relationship between Artemis and her hunting dog. In this statue, her tunic reaches the ground in a feminine manner. Like in Figure 4.1, she has an intense expression and a quiver on her back.

Voicing Artemis 31

Figure 4.3 Artemis housed in the Vatican Museum. Image by rjhuttondfw. Creative Commons – Attribution – ShareAlike 2.0 Generic - CC BY-SA 2.0. No changes made. [https://www.flickr.com/photos/rjhuttondfw/20654213895].

Figure 4.3 shows the crescent new moon on the crown of Artemis, the goddess of the new moon. The new moon represents transitions and new beginnings spiritually. As in Figures 4.1 and 4.2, she has a quiver on her back. However, in Figure 4.3, she is depicted in the act of hunting, as she is holding a bow, and her hunting dog is standing rather than sitting.

Artemis is a deadly huntress in poetry (Wilde, 1994). She is swift-footed. She is a virgin goddess in armour (Crowley, n.d.). She is a jealous maid in Wilde's prose (Wilde, 1881). According to Homer, Artemis delights in arrows (Richardson, Nicholas, & Homer, 1974). The festival Arkteia in Brauron, outside Athens, held every four years, was dedicated to the goddess. Children were taught to identify as 'bears' by wearing bearskins whilst performing initiation dances and holding young animals. This ritual helped young children learn to respect wild animals and nature (Hughes, 1990).

There are numerous psychological archetypes that Artemis represents and embodies. The Renaissance (sixteenth and seventeenth centuries) revived the interest in ancient Greek mythology, which continues to the present day. However, Artemis's function has taken on new psychological meanings. Cooper (1978) interprets Artemis as a universal (Jungian) archetype of freedom and independent femininity. Bolen (2014) interprets Artemis through Jungian archetypes and links them to women's collective unconscious. Alongside Athena and Hestia, Artemis is one of the virgin goddesses who symbolise women's independence.

Von Franz (1999) asserts that Artemis should be called by the Jungian term of the Self, representing the collective unconscious's entirety. Similarly, Strengell (2003) states that the Artemis archetype is related to female independence. As the goddess of hunting and the new moon, Artemis embodies the independent woman who decides to achieve her own goals in life (Bolen, 2014). She invokes the notion of freedom and the autonomous woman who lives life to her full potential according to her truth and goals. Artemis and the mother bear archetype represent modern women who choose not to be victims of circumstances and decide to speak up against inequality, sexism, and patriarchy (Bolen, 2014). Further, the archetypes of Artemis and Atalanta symbolise anyone who protests inequality and a patriarchal society, and the women's suffrage movement embodies these archetypes in action (Bolen, 2014). Bolen (2014) interprets Artemis as an archetype of sisterhood. She embodies strong women and the original feminist who stops rapists and seeks retribution against perpetrators. Anyone who works for justice and equality for women and children embodies the Artemis archetype (Bolen, 2014).

According to Strengell (2003) and Bolen (2014), Artemis is the goddess of the new moon. My Artemis aria 'Mi amor, la luna' is about the importance of the moon due to its phases via its waxing and waning. Artemis sends wild animals, such as the Calydon Boar, to destroy those who do not worship her in their yearly sacrifices to the gods and goddesses (Bolen, 2014). According to Strengell (2003), Artemis was the goddess of unwed girls and pregnant women. Hughes (1990) interprets Artemis as the educator of girls; Artemis also helped orphaned children. Atalanta was abandoned as a baby by her family, who were royals; her father, the king, left Atalanta to die in the wilderness because she was not a boy and was thus not a suitable heir to the throne. Artemis sent a bear to breastfeed Atalanta. One of Artemis's mythological totem animals is the mother bear, representing femininity (Bolen, 2014). Artemis' name may be etymologically related to 'arktos' ('bear' in ancient Greek) (Hughes, 1990, p. 193); the namesake is fascinating, as in Ancient Greece, prepubescent girls were taught to be little bears, embodying femininity. The 'arktoi' ('bears') were young girls protected from marriage who spent their time outdoors dressing as tomboys and learning how to be connected to nature from Artemis. According to Bolen (2014), the mother bear symbolises the protective nature of Artemis, as she protects young girls and mothers. Artemis helped girls transform into adults and represented the transition to womanhood. Thus, Budin (2015) interprets Artemis as the goddess of transitions.

Hughes (1990) also considers Artemis the goddess of conservation, as she was the protector of all flora and fauna. Her duality as a hunter and protector is represented in statues, such as the one in the Louvre (see Figure 4.1), which depicts her with one hand on the stag's head and the other ready to pull an arrow out of her quiver. As the goddess of forests, she embodies nature as purity and sacredness. In essence, Artemis is a conservationist (Hughes, 1990). She protects animals of the forest through bear cub societies. She is the goddess of the wild (Hughes, 1990).

Bolen (2014) interprets Artemis as the goddess of childbirth and midwifery; even though Artemis is one of the virgin goddesses, she aids other women with their births. Artemisia (Mugwort) is a herb named after her (Bolen, 2014) that was believed to aid in birth pangs when ingested during childbirth (Alberto-Puleo, 1978). Artemis became the goddess of midwifery because, when her mother, Leto, was giving birth, Artemis became a midwife for her twin brother Apollo, which was the most challenging birth in mythology.

In my libretto, when Orion declares that he will kill every animal in the world because he loves to hunt, Gaia (Mother Earth) sends a scorpion to kill him; Artemis is the goddess embodiment of Gaia. Killing Orion relates to Mother Earth's wrath on humanity (Bolen, 2014) on people or gods, in this case, who do not respect nature and transgress against it. The representations of Artemis were used in my opera, using nature as the virtual environment; the libretto explored the conservation of the planet as Mother Earth Gaia kills Orion to protect the animals. My choices in the libretto development were to highlight the protectress elements and goddess of the moon elements of the archetypes of Artemis; I chose the retelling of the myth where Gaia kills Orion instead of the version of the myth where Apollo challenges Artemis to shoot a target in the distance and results in Artemis shooting Orion's unrecognisable head by accident. The strength and independent archetypes of Artemis are highlighted in the libretto of 'Autumn Ayre' in which Artemis overcomes adversity after the death of Orion 'Winter has come, do not feel numb; you are full of life, you got through your strife'. The goddess of transitions and the new moon archetypes are highlighted in 'Mi amor, la luna' in the libretto when Artemis sings to the moon of the new moon seeing her through life's transitions

> All of the lights, come back on, you are feeling strong / I love the moon she sees me through / The darkest nights, and reignites, all of the lights / My love, the moon / The moon, my love / My love, the moon / The moon, my love.

The Artemis archetype of conservation and protectress of young girls is highlighted in the libretto in which Artemis sings, 'Zeus and Leto brought me to protect our forests and our daughters, all'.

Further, the goddess of transitions is highlighted using reborn in the libretto; being reborn is a signifier of transitions in life. Thus, I wrote in the libretto, 'Dusk turns to dawn, you are reborn, you are reborn'. The metaphor of leaves changing colour is a transitional metaphor, which I wrote in the libretto 'Leaves are turning hearts burning'. Artemis' connection to nature is highlighted through my use of words in the libretto referring to the beauty of the stars and Artemis rendering Orion in the stars after his death 'I render thee in the stars'. Bolen (2014) interprets Greek mythology as patriarchal. In the original mythological stories, Zeus rendered gods and goddesses into the stars; however, I took the artistic license to write into the libretto that Artemis rendered Orion into the star constellation named after him. Stars, forests, and nature are used in the libretto to signify Artemis as the goddess of the wilderness: 'Autumn as colourful as spring with leaves instead of poppies, red leaves like my love for the forest, yes! / My fellow deer and nymphs'. Deer are mentioned rather than the stag that is depicted in the statues of Artemis (see Figure 4.1) as deer are female versions of stags, and in this female-centric opera, I wanted to mention the deer. Nymphs were Artemis' companions; thus, I wrote them into the libretto. Further, Artemis' twin brother fell in love with a nymph in the opera Apollo and Daphne (Handel, 1710); hence, I used nymphs in the libretto of my opera to create cohesion with previous seminal operatic works. Zeus and Leto brought Artemis into the world to protect nature; she was a child of the wilderness and did what she wanted. Thus, I used this in the libretto

> I wish you light and love / And to all, all, yes, all people / Yes, I wish you, light and love. Yes! / love, love, I wish you, everything comes at the right time / Trust the future. Love, o, your love is as red as the flowers in the field / Love, o, love, as red as the flowers in the field. / Heavens, full of stars, we are all stars. / Millions of stars. / The stars sparkle like lights over the world. / Music is the love, like the stars in the sky, reliable, star clear night, splendour. / The child laughs and does what it wants.

4.1   Conclusion

In conclusion, in this chapter, I explored the creative ethos of my research, Greek mythology, its connection to opera, and Artemis's various archetypes and interpretations influenced the creative work. These elements influenced the narrative design of the opera. What I learnt about Artemis by adapting her to be an operatic character was that she is a strong role model for women who overcome adversity. Artemis embodies multiple archetypes that relate to the different seasons of a woman's life: the independent woman, the goddess of the moon and transitions, the goddess of equality, childbirth, and midwifery, and the goddess of protection and conservation. By adapting Artemis into an operatic character, I deliberately challenged operatic tropes depicting female opera characters dying due to the male protagonist's actions or journey. *Artemis* challenged operatic tropes discussed in Chapter 2, as Artemis survived adversity and lived to be an older woman, even when her lover Orion died in the elderly season of her life (Winter Duet). This research contributes to the scholarly perspectives I have discussed regarding women's representation, as discussed in Chapter 2. *Artemis* is an opera created as part of a canon of new opera works in which the female protagonist triumphs over adversity. In Chapter 5, I compare my AR and VR works through the lens of experience.

5 A Comparison of the AR and VR *Artemis* Works

This chapter explores the approaches to narrative design and world-building used to create the versions of *Artemis*, which influenced research question 1, 'How can self-experiential prototyping methodologies be used to create new opera experiences?'.

This chapter compares the three works and answers research question 2: What can be learnt by comparing three AR and VR opera creation processes based on the same operatic source material? Media examples have been included in text as examples of each of the works being discussed; these media examples are the creative portfolio component of this research project. Inspired by Kerslake (2002), I built upon the notion that a future opera model may be a video game. My opera is an artwork that draws upon XR artworks. However, my VR and AR works are different from games in terms of structure. Although interactive, they lack some elements that would take them into the game sphere. I drew upon the concept by Striner, Halpin, Röggla, and César Garcia (2021), who state, 'we envision a new form of VR opera that couples physical traditions with digital affordances' (p. 1).

Based on the same musical and thematic content, my opera had three forms – an AR experience and two VR experiences.

The AR opera was a live performance, AR visual layers were added by audience members when they scanned the QR codes (see media example 09). I developed the live AR performance with local Brisbane musicians, and the EyeJack smartphone app was used to deliver AR-based visual media. The live AR performance featured a mezzo-soprano, a tenor, a piano, and a synthesiser performing the 20-minute score. The audience members scanned a QR code and a poster printout of the target images and QR codes with their smartphones (see media example 05). These images were activated as a moving GIF screen in EyeJack (see media example 30). I painted the AR overlays in Tilt Brush (see media example 10). The visual AR overlays enhanced the performance by adding abstract art and horizontal re-sequencing to the interpretation of the performance (Sweet, 2015), which can increase immersion in the XR opera. The AR performance was executed in my PhD prototype as a live music performance plus art exhibition, in which participants scanned the

DOI: 10.4324/9781003642541-5

AR artwork in a random order. The viewers interacted with the art and music by walking around the performance venue in a choose your own adventure format of scanning the different AR posters. Due to the order of the visuals being individually selected by users roaming the performance hall, it influenced their understanding of what an AR opera was. The interaction with the art and music influenced the audience members' enjoyment of the live music, as the liveness made it a social event with interactive non-linear visuals (see media example 05).

These approaches catered to world-building.[1] The AR and VR environments were non-linear experiences; however, the music was mostly fixed. The non-linear nature is represented in the visual side of the work. The Oculus VR work employed Oculus Quest hand tracking (see media example 32). The ways that my VR opera used world-building were that the audience engaged with it through world augmentation, enabling movement around a virtual performance space. I created virtual worlds inspired by ancient Greece, using a Mount Olympus-looking skybox[2] in the Oculus[3] VR version. I also created my visual style with a similar colour palette for all three XR versions. In this chapter, in relation to what can be learnt by comparing three AR and VR opera creation processes based on the same operatic source material? I compare the outcomes of the creation of these three works to gain insights into the different processes of XR opera creation and their effectiveness in crafting XR opera.

The Oculus VR *Artemis* version was a first-person user experience. The effect is a computer game-like musical experience. Unity3D was used in the Oculus version; Unity3D is a game engine with properties, a skybox asset, and game object assets; I used Unity3D for VR development. This chapter documents the lenses I used during the Oculus *Artemis* experience design. Users mixed sounds in real time based on the proximity of their hands to virtual objects in the Oculus VR version of *Artemis*. Thus, the audience members controlled the playback order of different arias and duet according to the proximity of their hands to the four vases. Limitations of audio in the Oculus VR version included the fact that the audio was always stereo, which differed from the AR live performances in which the sound was ambisonic as it surrounded the listener; thus, there was a limited audio experience in the Oculus VR version. The act of singing live in the AR version was highlighted when the person was breathing in, the audience knew that the singer was about to sing in the live performance due to this visual feedback of the performer breathing in, in the Oculus VR version and YouTube VR version one did not have this visual feedback, as I, the creator, did not animate a singer. In the Oculus VR version of *Artemis*, the users entered a magical landscape in ancient Greece, floating in space above Mount Olympus, featuring four vases, trees, and a Greek temple. Each vase was associated with a horizontal re-sequenced composition (Sweet, 2015) aria or duet performed by a mezzo-soprano, a tenor, a piano, and a synthesiser. An aria or duet was played

38 Creating Opera Utilising Augmented Reality

back when the user walked towards a vase. The user's proximity to a vase changed the arias and duets' order, creating a non-linear experience.

Proximity interactivity in a virtual environment and immersion may be increased through virtual hands, hand tracking, and head tracking; I am not using these features to their full functionality in the playback of the three versions of *Artemis* (please see Hudson, Matson-Barkat, Pallamin, & Jegou, 2019). However, head tracking is used in both the Oculus and YouTube VR versions, whereas virtual gloves and hand tracking with virtual hands are used only in the Oculus VR version; it should be stated that users cannot grab objects in any of the versions of *Artemis*. In all the iteration versions of the interactive Oculus virtual reality (VR) opera, the composition itself was not changed; instead, the order of the compositions was passively interactive. The user's proximity to the vase assets changed the order of the playback of the arias, duets, and foley[4] elements. The composition process involved separating each aria and duet from the synth and foley elements.

The Oculus VR version was based on a non-linear experience that differed each time for each user. In contrast, the YouTube VR and AR versions were always the same in terms of linearity (see media example 31).

In the YouTube VR iterations, the experience is pre-recorded and linear. In iteration #2 of spring (see media example 17), the aria 'Licht und Liebe' is accompanied by visualisations of a tree with fresh green leaves. In the 26 December VR 2021 iteration (see media example 15), when the aria' Mi amor la luna' is played, the moon is visualised (see media example 15 timestamp 12:36). In autumn, the aria 'Autumn Ayre' is accompanied by visualisations of trees and foxes (see media example 15, timestamp 08:35). In winter,

Figure 5.1 Screenshots of the YouTube VR Artemis version (26 December 2021 iteration).

(*Continued*)

A Comparison of the AR and VR Artemis *Works* 39

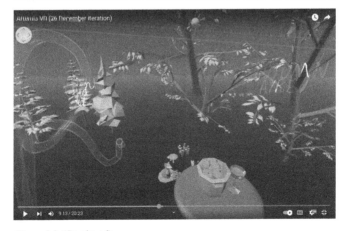

Figure 5.1 (Continued)

the aria 'Winter Duet' is accompanied by snowfall visualisations (see media example 15, timestamp 06:57) (see Figure 5.1). These seasonal visual elements created fluid transitions and visual consistency with the libretto. In iteration #3 of the YouTube VR experience, I introduced colour changes using Adobe Premiere Pro to add variation to the tree of life for each season (see media example 18). In regard to limitations of the work, the 26 December 2021 iteration of the YouTube VR *Artemis* (see media example 15) version had some issues. According to feedback from Altered Festival, the scene transitions in the form of different seasonal, virtual renders induced motion sickness. Lots of research has been conducted in VR and motion sickness (please see Dziuda, Biernacki, Baran, & Truszczyński, 2014). I rectified this by creating iteration #2 (see media example 17) using the scene of the green tree of life and discarding the other footage (see Figure 5.1). Altered Festival successfully exhibited iteration #2 (see media example 17).

In comparing the interactivity of the three versions, each version of *Artemis* was passive (see Table 7.1) in a different way. The YouTube VR version fits into category 1 of Table 7.1 (ghost without impact – observant passive). The only interactive element was head tracking, which changed according to where the audience member looked. Audience members were encouraged to walk around the space to change their perceptions of it, promoting a feeling of immersion, which may have resulted in a sense of presence. The Oculus version was a ghost with impact – observant active experience and fit into category 2 of Table 7.1 According to Dolan Paret's VR Storytelling Framework, the Oculus VR experience was a passive immersive experience (see Table 7.1).

This introduction highlighted the functional digital choices in creating the three versions. What was revealed in relation to research question 2 – 'What can be learnt by comparing three AR and VR opera creation processes based on the same operatic source material?' – was that the reflections from comparing the three versions included how each version of the opera was passive, they all used the same musical content, and the AR and VR experiences were all non-linear experiences. The conversations in the remainder of this chapter include narrative design choices used in my opera; narrative design is the story choices which an author makes in creating their work I have explained this through world creation choices and storyliving; this can encompass digital aspects and creative writing aspects. The narrative is opera, and for the Oculus VR version, it happens to be opera presented in Unity3D. Underpinning research that influenced my choices is also explored.

5.1 Narrative Design

Seminal theories have been put forth by Vallance and Towndrow (2022) and Bailenson (2018) regarding narrative design; these will be explored in this section. Similarly, Meadows (2003) has argued that various techniques increase the effectiveness of narrative design. My methodology for creating in VR for VR can be likened to the techniques used by the seminal painter Giotto who worked with perspective 'while putting the viewer in his own dimensional – or visual – perspective, he was also putting the viewer in his own emotional perspective' (Meadows, 2003, p. 8). By creating in VR for VR, I developed my distinct visual style. I painted in the VR goggles for all the YouTube VR versions using Tilt Brush. Through experimentation, I created a similar virtual colour palette for both the Oculus VR and YouTube VR versions. Viewers see the YouTube VR work from my perspective as I was painting it.

The use of seasons in the opera aimed to provide a narrative perspective of cohesively attaching the musical elements to the narrative of the myth of Artemis. The seasons represented the four stages of Artemis's life, and the visual themes of each season represented a different time frame of Artemis' life, namely birth, adolescence, middle age, and elderly years.

The author's and participant's perspectives are used in all three versions of *Artemis*, drawing upon interactive narrative: 'It's the human element of the perspective that's significant in stories' (Meadows, 2003, p. 29). My reinterpretation of the Artemis mythological story relates to how stories were reinterpreted during the Renaissance (Meadows, 2003). I conveyed my perspective as the creator to create a non-linear visual narrative (Meadows, 2003). From my perspective as a composer-maker, creating in VR for VR opera makes the narrative multidimensional and akin to a multiverse, which may engage the user emotionally and cognitively (Meadows, 2003). My interpretation of the story of Artemis is a new thematic perspective, in which she is a strong operatic character who overcomes adversity. Artemis triumphs over adversity and renders Orion in the stars.

Vallance and Towndrow (2022) proposed encouraging expansion and practical understanding in VR through narrative 'storyliving', in which effective experiences make the user feel embodied and present; I used storyliving through the enhancement of embodiment using hand tracking and proximity in the Oculus version. Thus, 'storytelling becomes storyliving' (Vallance & Towndrow, 2022, p. 2). In *Artemis*, I used 'storyworlding' (Bailenson, 2018), in which narrative (usually in a linear form) and gameplay are combined to create a new medium. The work of Vallance and Towndrow (2022) and Bailenson (2018) contributes to the fields of VR and AR opera and narrative design as the concepts of 'storyliving' and 'storyworlding' help creators put the audience members in the shoes of a first-person experiencer. This may in turn increase immersion in the narrative; these narrative design theories may expand current practices of increasing empathy and immersion in VR experiences. VR is the first medium that can create an autobiographical experience that is remembered like a personal memory (Bailenson, 2018). A narrative experience in VR is created through the psychological 'storification' process (Aylett &

Louchart, 2007, pp. 116–117), related to narrative psychology (Aylett & Louchart, 2007). Through these psychological means, storyliving and autobiographical memories are formed: 'Narrative Storyliving is thus not structured or pre-generated, but unfolds as the participant experiences the emerging, semi-authored virtual environment, providing imaginary visions of personal histories. ... Narrative Storyliving in VR becomes a form of self-representation' (Vallance & Towndrow, 2022, p. 4). All three versions of *Artemis* can create autobiographical memories through new emotional and cognitive experiences (Aylett & Louchart, 2007). Through storyliving, the user becomes more involved in the story.

In terms of interactivity, the Oculus VR experience mainly employs sonic interactivity, whereas the AR experience is mainly based on visual interactivity. However, free movement is possible in both. The YouTube VR and AR versions of *Artemis* fall into the non-participant influence category, as 'the author does not appear within the narrative experience but rather determines it with a control reaching variably down an abstraction hierarchy from overall theme, through abstract action sequences to details of character behaviour' (Aylett & Louchart, 2007, p. 119). Non-participant control means conventional authoring (see Table 5.1). The YouTube VR version of *Artemis* employed conventional authoring: I, the author, steered the user experience.

The Oculus version of *Artemis* fell into the non-participant control category: 'Non-participative influencing allowed the user to retain the objective aspects of the audience while simultaneously taking a degree of authorial responsibility for the overall narrative experience and typically interleaves interactive and non-interactive phases' (Aylett & Louchart, 2007, p. 119). I achieved this by combining the interactivity of the playback order of the arias or duets according to proximity with the non-interactivity of the structure of each aria and duet.

According to Bucher (2018), the creator must go into the creation process of an immersive narrative by asking who the audience is and what the purpose is of what the audience is to feel when walking away from the experience. In my case, the audience is anyone, and the purpose is to entertain and educate

Table 5.1 User Roles Across a Spectrum of Interactivity

Degree of Interactivity	Example
None	Conventional audience/spectator.
Non-participant control	Conventional authoring.
Non-participant influence	Forum theatre spect-actors; Deus ex machina; many God games.
Participant control points	Branching narratives.
Freely participating character	LARP, emergent narrative.

Source: Adapted from Aylett and Louchart (2007, p. 119).

through a female-centric opera. In the Oculus VR version, sound objects are attached to four ancient Greek vases. An aria or duet begins when the user is near a vase. Sound is triggered by proximity, not by touch. Nothing else happens apart from the playback order of the musical pieces changing (see media example 27, timestamp 0:57). As the user wanders through the VR world, natural foley sounds are played to immerse the user in the virtual world, depending on their proximity to a red tree. The user is teleported directly into the middle of the four vases (see media example 19). The Oculus VR work leverages musical interactivity through horizontal re-sequencing, as the user changes the music structure in audio file chunks (Sweet, 2015) in the 3D space in a through-composed form that is true to traditional opera, in which each aria and duet always has the same structure and listening experience. Opera is through-composed, meaning it does not have moving sonic elements in the way that game music has re-sequenced elements related to the gameplay (Sweet, 2015). I chose to employ this simple structure, as opposed to a structure with variable music or music revealed through more complex in-world actions, to replicate the form of traditional opera. In gameplay experiences, the music changes through every turn (see branching narratives in Table 5.1), whereas the Oculus VR version of my opera provides experiential entertainment. I effectively built a virtual stage or public square for my opera (see media example 19).

When comparing the visuals of the different versions, the visual structure and duration of the AR GIFs in the AR performance drew upon non-linear sequence; contrastingly, each aria and duet was through-composed. Thus, the musical structure and playback of the different instruments in the arias and duets did not change.

In the AR work, the QR code and target images were printed on a poster to convey the story of the Greek goddess Artemis and the god Orion floating above the clouds in ancient Greece (see Figure 5.2).

Figure 5.2 Target images and QR code screenshots for the AR version of Artemis.

5.2 World-Building

In the Oculus and YouTube VR productions, I employed world-building. I built the entire world and everything inside it as a virtual environment. My AR opera was in a physical location overlaid by AR components as a narrative intervention to create new meaning.

The parts of traditional opera I aimed to transfer were the aria and duet compositional structures. The musical composition was the same between the three versions. The difference was in the playback order of the arias and duets. In the Oculus VR version, the order of each aria and duet was mediated by technology alongside the story layer of the work. The sound design and foley were non-notated, whereas the arias and duets were notated. The work's soundtrack was the score, and the act of wandering in the virtual environment was the performance itself. The choice to use simple music was due to the opera's narrative design; it was composed to match up with the mythological seasons of Artemis' life.

World creation enhanced the narrative design by visually highlighting the mythological story of Artemis through Greek assets and the choice of the Greek Mount Olympus skybox in Unity3D, which influenced opera as the visual was highly important for the cohesion of the Gesamtkunstwerk, where expensive physical visual sets were used by Richard Wagner in Bayreuth; I used virtual visual sets to enhance the mythological story. By crafting multiple versions of *Artemis* for different XR mediums, I explored the creation of 3D passive immersive experiences, which impacted my practice as a composer by bringing it into dialogue with the adjacent practices of sound implementation and game development (see Figures 6.3–6.8). In the process, I learnt the game development practices of iteration and prototyping. Learnings from my project were that the narrative mythology story choices influenced my virtual set design in Unity3D, as I composed the music before creating the world. The different XR versions contributed to these learnings due to the need to become flexible and adaptable to multiple software and hardware platforms, which, in turn, made me a more versatile, all-around creator.

Narrative design for each season of Artemis' life was included; the narrative of spring and the birth of Artemis was the first story element of the opera. The Vase_Amphora was narratively at the beginning of Artemis's life. The user's proximity to the vase triggered the playback of the 'Licht und Liebe' duet, sung by Zeus and Leto on the joyous occasion of Artemis's birth (see media example 27).

In the narrative of the later years of Artemis's life, her hair was white as snow. She lost her lover Orion when he declared that he would kill every animal in the world, and Mother Earth Gaia sent a scorpion to kill him for his boasting. When the user was near the hydria vase, the 'Winter Duet' was heard, in which Artemis and Orion sang about their love. Orion was killed, and Artemis rendered Orion in the stars, forming the Orion constellation.

I used audio source setups in Unity3D, employed the vase assets, and set up the session logically (see media example 26).

These were the frameworks I employed to frame my opera; I used Unity3D for the Oculus version of the interactive 'Mi amor la luna'; this aria is sung by Artemis in her adolescence and is related to summer. The aria was played when the user was close to the volute krater vase (see media example 26). Artemis sang about her love for the moon, which always saw her through the darkest nights and reignited her spirit.

I used nature sound foley; I used the sound of the cuckoo, an important bird in ancient Greek mythology. The cuckoo was one of Hera's totem animals, and Zeus took the form of a cuckoo to trick Hera whilst courting her. I set up the audio; I mapped the foley to the red tree asset, which I imported from Tilt Brush's Poly library and recoloured in Unity3D (see media example 26).

A skybox was the background or backdrop asset as the virtual environment in the game engine development software Unity3D; I chose a Greek skybox with mountain ranges to go cohesively with the narrative theme of the gods and goddesses of ancient Greece living on Mount Olympus; it was a creative decision to use the snow-covered mountain skybox. I used this skybox narratively to go with the myth of Artemis. All the gods and goddesses lived on Mount Olympus; the skybox fit this theme with the mountain ranges (see media example 19).

I used a specific hierarchy I learnt from Unity3D tutorials for the hierarchy of the game engine setup for the Oculus VR version of *Artemis* (see media example 26).

The frameworks I employed for the iterative case study of the Oculus version are listed in Table 6.1; I learnt from these examples how to reflect upon an iterative self-experiential prototyping process through journal entries that highlighted problem statements and key takeaways from my process. The rationale behind *Artemis* is that the seasons reflect nature, and the environment is a medium. This theme is realised visually and sonically in a magical virtual environment (see media example 19).

My work is helpful for other creators who want to create assets and models of visual experiences in Tilt Brush. I brought in my perspective by prototyping in VR in real time, then importing my models into Unity3D and deploying the built virtual environment to the VR headset, resulting in a cyclic artistic process (with research question 1, 'How can self-experiential prototyping methodologies be used to create new opera experiences?') for creating new Oculus VR musical works. It is also helpful for other creators to know that social presence can be enhanced by using virtual hands mapped to the user's real hands, called hand presence. Spatial imagery and immersive 3D sounds created an intimate sense of presence and aided in spatial navigation (Spillers, 2017). Striner, Halpin, Röggla, and César Garcia's (2021) research aligned with what I am doing with affordances to create immersive VR opera for new audiences, 'Using these findings, we envision a new form of opera that couples physical traditions with digital affordances' (Striner, Halpin, Röggla, & César Garcia, 2021, p. 311).

5.3 Conclusion

In conclusion, the learnings from this chapter are directly related to research question 2 – 'What can be learnt by comparing three AR and VR opera creation processes based on the same operatic source material?' – by comparing the three versions.

This experimental action-based research project provided significant insights into the process of world-building in the context of VR opera. The implications for other creators are that composing is at the forefront of this methodology – the composition is innovating VR opera, and VR is not renewing the opera.

By employing self-experiential prototyping and examining creative processes through various perspectives, I sought to explore potential methods that other creators could apply to their own work.

Another key finding was that interactivity was important for building presence in the Oculus VR experience. Using my findings of world-building and creation, I envisioned a new form of XR opera that combined musical and digital affordances to immerse audience members. By learning how to utilise world-building in opera creation, I understood its broader implications, such as creating experiences that do not induce motion sickness through too much movement in the frames. The implications of these findings are that my research furthers the concept put forward by Sheil and Vear (2012) of digital opera being used to 'renew the operatic canon' (p. 5), as I have created interdisciplinary digital opera which fuses through-composed music with new XR technologies. Thus, this research contributes to the wider academic conversation about VR and opera, primarily extending the concept of digital opera.

The implications of the findings from research question 2 – 'What can be learnt by comparing three AR and VR opera creation processes based on the same operatic source material?' – are that the comparison of different mediums can help future digital opera practitioners prototype new works. The findings from this chapter relate directly to the research questions, as I highlighted a prototype scenario in which the representation of a fixed opera composition is reshaped by the medium used: Oculus VR, YouTube VR, and EyeJack AR.

The implications from these findings are that using the lenses can help creators shape an experience and reflect on their creative processes. The lenses are inspired by Schell (2020), and my reference to lenses is the figures of the processes I created. These lenses can be used as different angles of reflection in the making process. Accordingly, future practitioners can look at my three versions through different eyes. Future digital opera creators and practitioners can compare the different mediums, which helped me formulate a way of creating an original opera that was experienced by audiences in diverse ways. Attention given to the different ways of utilising new technologies can help future digital opera creatives rethink canonical opera creation.

Having discussed the lessons learned and their implications in this chapter, the following section will delve into the specific prototyping processes utilised in the creation of the XR opera, *Artemis*.

Notes

1 For VR.
2 A skybox is a background asset in Unity3D, it is used to set the scene and make the experience a colourful immersive scene rather than just a dark room experience.
3 An Oculus Quest is a VR headset goggle set, it differs from the HTC Vive headset due to the brand and technical specifications.
4 Foley: sound design (footsteps, water, wind, birdcalls).

6 Prototyping an Iterative Process

This chapter explores the outcomes and learnings obtained from my research in relation to research question 1, 'How can self-experiential prototyping methodologies be used to create new opera experiences?', including the development of new models and processes which were developed as findings from research question 1, 'How can self-experiential prototyping methodologies be used to create new opera experiences?' Table 6.1 specifically highlights a methodology in relation to research question 1, 'How can self-experiential prototyping methodologies be used to create new opera experiences?'. Figures and Tables are included to convey my findings visually. Two different methodologies are used: an approach that starts with a problem statement and a brainstorming-led approach. The reasoning behind the two methods being used was that I conducted self-experiential prototyping in multiple ways to glean new insights into XR opera creation.

The process of self-experiential prototyping described in this book is grounded in human-computer interaction (HCI), user experience, and interaction design. The underpinning theories are human-centred and draw on those put forth by Benyon (2013), who argues that usability is an essential aspect of software engineering. Web designers should focus on usability to create user-friendly web designs. Product developers should focus on inclusive designs, and engineers should be trained to understand people by creative individuals who understand the limits of software engineering (Benyon, 2013). According to Benyon (2013), understanding and using the PACT (people, activities, contexts, technologies) framework is essential for designing interactive systems and experiences. Further, 'designers should strive to achieve a harmony between the needs of different people who undertake activities in contexts using technologies' (Benyon, 2013, p. xvii). Benyon (2013) further states that designing interactive technologies entails understanding 'the variety inherent in the four elements of PACT' (p. 26); this includes designing systems for a variety of people, people with different heights, body weights, abilities, disabilities, wheelchair users, and near and short-sightedness. Accordingly, I designed the AR performance to be wheelchair-accessible and child height friendly by putting up the AR target images at three different heights.

For the design of the AR performance, I followed the premise that 'interaction involves an exchange but is not limited to computer systems. In the realm of user experience, this concept of mutual effect implies that interaction must be considered within a context or environment shared between system and user' (Hartson & Pyla, 2012, p. 6). User experience is an interaction between two parties, a computer and a human, i.e., HCI:

> Given the many different definitions of 'interaction' in the HCI literature, we turned to the English definition of the word: mutual or reciprocal action, effect, or influence, as adapted from Dictionary.com. So, the interaction involves an exchange but is not limited to computer systems. In the realm of user experience, this concept of mutual effect implies that interaction must be considered within a context or environment shared between system and user.
>
> (Hartson & Pyla, 2012, p. 6)

In summary, user experience is an interaction between a computer and a human. Next, I cover the concept of prototyping UX design. Hartson and Pyla (2012) define user experience as the whole experience outcome which arises from a user interacting with the product; user experience encompasses usability, practicality, emotional effects, and the memory of the experience.

Norman (2013) argues that collaboration between humans and machines is vital to creating successful, usable experiences and products. Norman (2013) further states that design thinking entails that design must be iterative; firstly, the creator must develop the problem statement to be solved; secondly, designers broaden their views and do not choose a problem statement straight up. Design thinking encompasses the human-centred design model and the double-diamond diverge-converge design model: human-centred design is relevant to prototyping new products and software applications (Norman, 2013):

> Human-centred design (HCD) is the process of ensuring that people's needs are met, that the resulting product is understandable and usable, that it accomplishes the desired tasks, and that the experience of use is positive and enjoyable. HCD is a procedure for addressing these requirements, but with an emphasis on two things: solving the right problem, and doing so in a way that meets human needs and capabilities.
>
> (Norman, 2013, p. 219)

There are two elements to design thinking: the double-diamond approach, developed by Stanford University (Norman, 2013). The double-diamond model for design helps one create human-centred design applications (Norman, 2013). The human-centred design process comprises four steps. Firstly, observation; secondly, idea generation (Norman, 2013). Thirdly, prototyping, and lastly, testing; Norman (2013) states, 'These four activities are iterated…

they are repeated over and over, with each cycle yielding more insights and getting closer to the desired solution' (p. 222). This iterative process is like Schell's problem statement and the loop process discussed previously.

The stages for Artemis are the built AR and VR environments, which contribute to the overall musical experience (Hamilton, 2019). The high frame rates of VR made the creation and virtual staging of the immersive opera easier. Regarding HCI, the participant is a first-person experiencer, choosing where to look and walk in the virtual and physical spaces.

6.1 Self-Experiential Prototyping for Opera Creation

The prototypes contributed to the overall musical experience, as I experimented with the best ways of integrating the audio into each prototype, resulting in the most comfortable musical user experience. The exploration of research question 1 – 'How can self-experiential prototyping methodologies be used to create new opera experiences?' – resulted in the development of a personalised aesthetic for opera creation. The novelty lies in the making of the experience rather than in the future of XR opera, which is beyond the scope of this thesis. I tried various methods to create a new digital post-classical Gesamtkunstwerk (Sheil & Vear, 2012) opera. Creating a post-classical XR opera required acquiring professional game design and development skills. I used paper prototyping and sketching and learned how to conduct 'fast and dirty' prototyping to create new music opera experiences (see Figure 6.3). Through this journey, I developed multiple processes for creating new XR opera experiences by implementing prototyping workflows for Oculus VR (see Figure 6.5), YouTube VR (see Figure 6.6), and AR (see Figure 6.7).

Prototyping entails making something better and refining it until it is ready for release. From my autoethnographic perspective, prototyping encompassed the entire experience creation, including music recording, filming, and post-production editing in Adobe Premiere Pro. It also included visual sculpting and thinking about the music implementation whilst I was conducting self-experiential testing using the VR headset. To encompass the breadth of the work, I created macro-relationship models for each prototyping process. These models explain how I achieved the desired outcomes – enjoyable user experiences. My personal experiences with the tools Unity3D, Tilt Brush, Adobe Premiere Pro, and EyeJack Creator helped me develop my identity as a self-experiential prototyping expert. By employing these technologies, I created unique processes and frameworks for XR opera creation, which would not have been realised without these new technologies. My prototyping work addresses my research question 'How can self-experiential prototyping methodologies be used to create new opera experiences?' as it gives step-by-step processes and diagrams of how I undertook my theoretical framework for XR opera creation.

Prototyping an Iterative Process 51

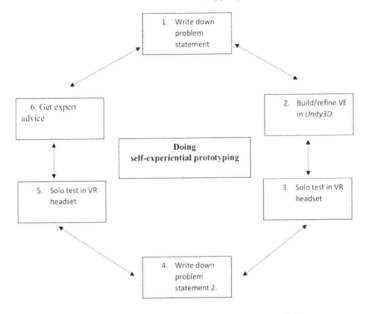

Figure 6.1 My self-experiential prototyping: an iterative cyclic model.

The steps for self-experiential prototyping are explored in this thesis through figures, highlighting how others may create new VR opera experiences (see Figure 6.2). The Oculus VR version of my opera and my autoethnographic prototyping method employed iterative models. A workflow for other creators has been created in this thesis to visualise the same process viewed through two different lenses to explain how self-experiential prototyping methodologies can guide composer-makers in creating new works.

I have used figures to detail my journey through each stage of the cyclic process of self-experiential prototyping (see Figure 6.1). I used steps to highlight my process; in step 1, I wrote down a problem statement. In step 2, I created the software or, for the second iteration, refined the virtual environment in Unity3D. I then assessed the experience by solo testing using the VR headset (step 3). Whilst immersed in the experience, I found some things that could have worked better. I then wrote down a second problem statement (step 4) and moved between steps 4 and 5 to fix the problem. Once I was content with addressing the problem statements, I created a 'build' of the experience in Unity3D and asked an expert to test it using a VR headset. The expert then provided feedback on elements that I needed to fix; the experts were my PhD supervisors, who are experts in music and architecture. This feedback was then used as a new problem statement for the next testing iteration, which led back to step 1.

52 Creating Opera Utilising Augmented Reality

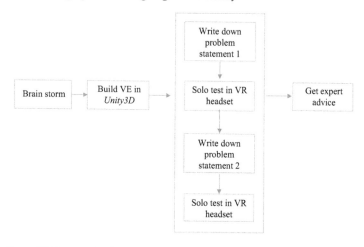

Figure 6.2 Structured and sequential self-experiential process steps for Oculus Quest prototyping.

According to Smith and Dean (2009), academic research and creative practice are inextricable aspects of knowledge creation. I created a figure to demonstrate how my research relates to Smith and Dean's iterative cyclic web model, in which practice and research occur continuously (see Figure 6.2). Continuous knowledge creation and testing cyclically encompassed my entire research project. This creative practice resulted in new models and processes that can be used in other makers' and scholars' research (see Figure 6.2).

I, the composer-maker, tested a model for designing an XR opera by implementing self-experiential prototyping in a structured way (see Figure 6.2). I used steps; for example, in step 1, I brainstormed the overall aesthetic of the opera through visualisation and note-taking. I then moved directly from brainstorming to making a rough virtual environment in Unity3D (step 2), moving between steps 1 and 2 to visualise and execute my idea. After building a prototype, I wrote down a problem statement (step 3a) that needed to be solo tested. After solo testing using the VR headset (step 3b), I identified a new problem and wrote down problem statement 2 (step 3c). I then moved between this step and the next to fix the problem in Unity3D. I then conducted solo testing using the VR headset again to see if the problem was resolved. I then created a 'build' of the Unity3D project and moved on to obtain expert advice.

One process I used began with writing down a problem statement (see Figure 6.1), whereas another process I used began with brainstorming (see Figure 6.2). I used both approaches in my project. Brainstorming is a broad-brush approach to experience creation, whereas a problem statement implies that the maker has already begun testing. I used figures to highlight my perspective as a solo creator responsible for all development stages (see Figures 6.1 and

6.2). I, the maker, went directly from brainstorming to making a novel rapid prototyping method (see Figure 6.2). I used self-experiential prototyping to fix problems, and my models helped to structure my prototyping process (see Figures 6.1 and 6.2). I walked around the Unity3D build and moved my head to assess the user experience (see Figures 6.1 and 6.2).

As part of my mixed methodology, I kept an autoethnographic journal for the Oculus VR version, writing problem statements (Schell, 2020). The autoethnographic journal was a free-form journal. I used the six steps of the iterative loop as headings (see Table 6.1). I recorded the steps to create successful builds, including the elements used in each prototype iteration. In the next prototype iteration, I documented the steps for creating materials and wrote down issues and steps to be taken in the following prototyping session. The relationship of the problem statements to the design process helped me keep track of the necessary changes to make better iterations. I used a bottom-up approach in my visual prototyping for the Oculus VR version, and I started with various skyboxes, then I added in assets; the assets of Greek vases and temples added cultural relevance and cultural aspects, which were linked back to the narrative design of the opera being set in ancient Greece. The logarithmic audio setting in the spatialiser plugin in Unity3D worked well in prototyping, as the audio was more experiential for the user (see Figure 6.7). The reasoning behind choosing the final skybox for the Oculus VR version was that I decided to use the skybox because it did not leave the user in a dark experience; it may have led the user to feel immersed and have the user feel as if they had travelled to Greece. The method for the Oculus VR version of prototyping was that I composed first, then I created the visuals in Tilt Brush using the Poly Library and recolouring them in Unity3D; I then combined these with the Unity3D Asset Store assets from the Greek temple asset pack and Greek vases asset pack.

The methods I employed in this thesis included drawing upon Schell's (2020) theories to create my models of self-experiential prototyping. I also drew on methodologies for risk mitigation in game development. The idea behind risk mitigation is that the creator tries to eliminate or reduce risks related to game enjoyment by improving the game mechanics and the overall game experience. An example is the creation of numerous Oculus VR prototypes throughout my PhD research during 2020–2023 (see prototyping videos and screenshots on my website; link in the appendix).

My design method entailed prototyping various virtual Greek environments in Unity3D. I composed the music first in 2020; then, I worked on creating visuals. This methodology is consistent with how the light and sound architect Xenakis draws inspiration from music and mathematical formula visualisations to create architectural structures (Xenakis, 1992). I drew on Xenakis's light and sound architectural techniques to develop the Oculus version of my opera, fusing virtual visual and sonic elements to create a set in ancient Greece. I chose Xenakis, as he was both Greek and a computer musician. Xenakis (1992) created a light bulb and laser work by effectively using the relationship between light and sound. Each light bulb emitted light of a different frequency, which corresponded to a different pitch in the musical composition. Similarly, in prototyping Artemis, the proximity of the spatialised audio to the user's virtual hands in the Oculus VR version was based on the relationship between light (visuals) and sound.

I used journal entries to develop the Oculus VR version of Artemis; this entailed using various problem statements and reflection stages, including four to five stages of idea generation, initial development, reflection and refinement, finalisation, testing, review, and conclusions; I used these journal entries to document the iterative Oculus version creation process (see Table 6.1).

In an early prototype, I used each cube for narrative purposes (see media example 21). Each cube was related to a different season. The white cube was related to winter. The green cube was related to spring. The yellow cube was related to summer. The red cube was related to autumn. These relationships go with the narrative design of the opera, in which the four different arias and duets correspond to a different season.

I imported Poly trees as the trees represented different seasons in my narrative; the colour of each tree went together with a different season and thus a different aria or duet; this is similar to the 15 April 2021 prototype; however, instead of cubes the different seasons are represented as different trees, and each aria or duet's audio source is mapped to each corresponding tree depending on colour and colour connotations to different seasons (see media example 23). The 21 April 2021 prototype was the first prototype in which I imported temple assets and vases from the Unity3D store and combined these with the tree assets I painted in Tilt Brush, which I recoloured (see media example 23).

The reason for choosing the skybox was that it looked like a peak of Mount Olympus rather than the barren landscape of Athens; this goes together with my narrative design; the vase assets I chose from the Unity3D asset store were titled Greek, hence why I chose them to go with the narrative of the mythology of Artemis' life. The conjunction of this skybox and the added Greek vases was to create an ancient Greek Mount Olympus environment; the vases ensured that it went with the narrative and that users would not mistake it for the Swiss Alps (see media example 24).

The design method used for building the Oculus VR version was having the screens left and right, the game view on the right-hand side and the scene view on the left (see media example 25).

Whereas, for the YouTube VR version iterations, I used Tilt Brush painting software, which allows the artist to be immersed in a 3D environment whilst painting. I created this 360° medium (i.e., the YouTube VR version), filmed the path in Tilt Brush, and exported my work. Tilt Brush allowed me to paint assets from the beginning in an iterative process, as I employed quick and dirty prototyping (Schell, 2020) through trial and error. In prototype iteration #3

Table 6.1 Journal Entries for the Oculus VR Iterations

	15 April VR Test 2021	20 April Prototype 2021	21 April Prototyping Test 1 2021	21 April Prototyping Test 2 2021	21 April Prototyping Test 3 2021	17 May Prototype 2021
Idea generation	I added audio sources to the game object cubes in Unity3D to correspond to foley from each season: 1 Winter is a white cube; the audio source is 'Waves_Wind'. 2 Spring is a green cube; the audio source is 'cuckoo_bird_call'. 3 Summer is a yellow cube, the audio source is 'EQed Bees and Cicadas'. 4 Autumn is a red cube; the audio source is 'SFX leaves falling for Autumn of Artemis'. I used Spatial Blend 3D, logarithmic, Maximum Distance 50.					
Initial development	Problem question 1: Can the user pick up the cubes and hear the corresponding audio file?	I built a green plane and added four Greek vase assets at each corner of the plane.	Problem statement 1: When I move my head using the Oculus Quest headset, the scene moves as well.	Problem statement 1: The audio is not reactive.	Test 3.1 The experience is enjoyable.	I successfully implemented the virtual hands after troubleshooting.

(Continued)

Prototyping an Iterative Process 55

Table 6.1 (Continued)

	15 April VR Test 2021	20 April Prototype 2021	21 April Prototyping Test 1 2021	21 April Prototyping Test 2 2021	21 April Prototyping Test 3 2021	17 May Prototype 2021
		a skybox called 'Greek skybox' from the asset store, and an Artemis temple in the middle of the plane, this was an early iteration, in which the temple was placed in the middle. The user must walk towards the vases to hear the four arias and duets.				Problem statement 1: I found that the virtual hands faced the user's body upwards over the physical forearm; thus, they faced the wrong way. To rectify this, I followed the steps outlined on the Oculus developer's website (Meta, 2022).
Reflection and refinement	The build was successful. However, the 'ControllerModels' VR scene was the inside of a room, which was quite claustrophobic and not as expected.	Head tracking is not set up correctly in Unity3D.	To solve this problem, I looked at the elements in the VR demo scene 'ControllerModels' and compared them with	To address the problem statement,	Problem statement 2: The 'Autumn Ayre' aria name text model conflicts with the 'Vase_Amphora [1]' model.	Problem statement 2: I felt as if I was hovering in space

Prototyping an Iterative Process 57

Table 6.1 (Continued)

	15 April VR Test 2021	23 April Prototype 2021	21 April Prototyping Test 1 2021	21 April Prototyping Test 2 2021	21 April Prototyping Test 3 2021	17 May Prototype 2021
	I made the top cube from wooden material in Unity3D. I am testing it again with the top cube (which is essentially the ceiling) as an open skybox material so that the user does not feel boxed in.	I built the scene in Unity3D and then solo tested it using the Oculus Quest headset.	my custom-built project. I realised that I had an extra 'OVRCameraRig', which I did not need, as the 'OVRPlayer Controller' includes a child 'OVRCameraRig'. I solved the problem by removing the 'OVRCameraRig' from the hierarchy and building the scene.	I looped the audio source and used Spatial Blend 3D and Maximum Distance 50 settings.	Fix this by moving the vase asset. Add audio sources to each vase. Problem statement 2: The Tilt Brush text conflicts with the vase asset. Fix the scale of 'Untitled_0' (my FBX model created in Tilt Brush) to make it bigger so that it does not clash with the vase asset.	when I changed the plane ratio to 1 × 1 × 1. To rectify this, I moved the 'OVRPlayer' game object to the centre of the plane in Unity3D.
Finalisation	This build is much better, as the sky is expansive, and the 3D sound works well with the spatialisation		It works. I can successfully walk around with head tracking and locomotion. The 3D sounds work well,	I moved the vases, to line up with the running cursive which I painted in Tilt Brush,	Test 3.2 It looks excellent scale-wise. Problem statement: The experience begins with the user clashing with a tree model.	Problem statement 3: I tried using a dial from the 'VR Buttons and Levers' pack from the Unity3D asset store.

(*Continued*)

Table 6.1 (Continued)

15 April VR Test 2021	20 April Prototype 2021	21 April Prototyping Test 1 2021	21 April Prototyping Test 2 2021	21 April Prototyping Test 3 2021	17 May Prototype 2021
triggering the audio playback through proximity to the cubes and the crossfading of the music pieces.		and the virtual environment is realistic, with the 'Greek skybox' from the asset store filled with snow-covered hills and blue skies mottled with clouds.	to match the name of each aria.	I fixed this by moving the 'OVRPlayer Controller' asset to the middle of the vase area. *Test 3.3* Problem statement: The user starts in a position that is still too close to the tree models. I moved the 'OVRPlayer Controller' again. I added a high-level audio source of cuckoo bird calls as an ambient environment foley. I also added audio recordings from an opera rehearsal as a mock-up until the complete opera is recorded.	This caused build errors due to compiler errors in the scripting. To rectify this, I deleted the asset package and mapped the synth instrumental to the trees.

(Continued)

Prototyping an Iterative Process 59

Table 6.1 (Continued)

	15 April VR Test 2021	20 April Prototype 2021	21 April Prototyping Test 1 2021	21 April Prototyping Test 2 2021	21 April Prototyping Test 3 2021	17 May Prototype 2021
Testing, review, conclusions	I am changing the 3D 'grabbles' game objects to have different colours. A key learning from this prototype is the limitation of the 'ControllerModels' integration scene, as the user is inside a cube, which is not in line with my open-world VR experience plan. Therefore, I will try my custom-built scene using the 'OVRCameraRig', 'Plane', and 'OVRPlayerController' game objects.	Whilst testing, the virtual environment moved with my head. The head tracking was not set up correctly. The conclusion to take to the next prototyping stage is that.	I edited the scene for testing to have the temple on a realistic scale. It is best to set the plane at 2 × 2 × 2. This is a learning to take to my next prototype. I moved the vases closer to the temple.	A key learning was learning how to accurately match up the arias with visual models to create audiovisual cohesion in the virtual environment.	Test 3.4 Everything works as it should. It is a realistic interactive VR experience. Problem statement: There are no virtual hand controllers/ gloves in the experience. These will be added in the next prototype.	Problem statement: The FMOD aria events may be clashing sonically with one another. The VR experience works successfully untethered. Tracking works well, and I can see the virtual hands. The hands pass through the virtual objects.

(*Continued*)

Table 6.1 (Continued)

15 April VR Test 2021	20 April Prototype 2021	21 April Prototyping Test 1 2021	21 April Prototyping Test 2 2021	21 April Prototyping Test 3 2021	17 May Prototype 2021
There are a Greek temple asset and Greek vase assets. The vase assets trigger audio. There are four trees. I changed their material to correspond to each season. Each tree is at a different corner of the plane. When the user walks towards a tree, the corresponding aria is played. The user must collect vases to hear natural sounds from each season. This is an early iteration in which the proximity aspects were the opposite to future iterations. Each aria or duet is mapped to a different coloured tree.	I need to reread the online Oculus developer manual regarding headtracking	A key learning from this prototype is that the vases are too far apart. The plane's 3 × 3 × 3 scale is a bit too large for a room-scale experience. I will reduce it to 1 × 1 × 1 and test this smaller scale. However, 1 × 1 × 1 may induce vertigo, as the plane may be too small with the Greek mountain skybox for people who are afraid of heights. I will try this scale in the next prototyping phase.	The user will walk towards each vase and written cursive to hear one of the four arias/duets. The audio sources are mapped to the following: 'Licht und Liebe' (duet) is mapped to 'Vase_Amphora'. 'Mi amor la luna' (aria) is mapped to 'Vase_Volutekrater,' 'Autumn Ayre' (aria) is mapped to 'Vase_Amphora [1]', and the		I learnt to make sure that the SteamVR app was running on the computer to track and play the experience in Oculus. The sound works well, reflecting the narrative intention and spatialisation. The arias and duets are triggered accurately according to the user's proximity to a vase, and the music crossfading is appealing. A limitation is that the experience works best tethered.

Prototyping an Iterative Process 61

Table 6.1 (Continued)

15 April VR Test 2021	20 April Prototype 2021	21 April Prototyping Test 1 2021	21 April Prototyping Test 2 2021	21 April Prototyping Test 3 2021	17 May Prototype 2021
This prototype is not quite right. The problem is that there is one compiler error in a C# script in the 'DreamForestTree' package' asset regarding the repainting of the leaves. I created my materials and repainted the leaves of each tree. I deleted the 'DreamForestTree' assets. I created another prototype with the 'ControllerModels' Unity3D sample scene by moving the five cubes apart to create a more open-world virtual environment. The key learning was that this was not the game aesthetic I was seeking, as I wanted to use vases rather than cubes to create a more authentic ancient Greek world. This is the conclusion to take to the next prototype.			'Winter Duet' is mapped to 'Vase_Hydria'.		

(see media example 18), I painted the Tree of Life to represent Artemis's life. I added colour changes to the Tilt Brush recording in Adobe Premiere Pro; these colour changes were used to add variation to the recording and marry the visual to the theme of the libretto of each aria and duet. I chose blue tones for winter. I made the Tilt Brush recording black and white to highlight the nightscape for the aria 'Mi amor la luna' and added orange tones to the recording for autumn in Adobe Premiere Pro. The YouTube VR version is an online experience exhibited at multiple festivals, including Altered Festival 2022 in Chicago (see media example 17) and XR: WA 2022 in Perth (see media example 17). Media example 15 won the 2022 Best in Queensland Award at the Queensland XR Festival. The YouTube VR version is practical, as anyone can experience it for free on YouTube (see media example 18). You can watch my walkthrough video to see the processes behind creating the YouTube VR version (see media example 31).

Proof of concept videos are included in the portfolio (see media example 05, media example 07). The audience is drawn in virtually using the phone app to see the AR overlays (see media example 09), and I painted the AR overlays in Tilt Brush (see media example 10). A walkthrough video includes the processes and software I employed to create the AR version (see media example 30). The AR version was the most engaging for me as a composer, as performers attract people.

According to Clément (1988), opera is 'balanced in the clouds, in circle after circle … [it] unites with the secret of the gods … on the carved stage where an opera audience watches us through a giant piercing eye' (p. 6). I used this cloud metaphor in one of the target images for the AR version, painting clouds over Olympus, the home of the Greek gods and goddesses.

The next section expounds the various prototyping processes, which are visual outputs of my research project. Each figure explains out the step-by-step processes, which were developed as findings from research question 1, 'How can self-experiential prototyping methodologies be used to create new opera experiences?'.

Figure 6.3 outlines the process of prototyping the music for my XR opera. First, I composed the score using the digital scoring software Finale. I then experimented with the Canonic Utilities function, which I used instead of traditional (manual) orchestration techniques. My compositional process constituted an additional layer of technological intervention. I used these digital functions to rapidly prototype the composition by changing the modality for seamless transitions between each aria and duet and trying different harmonisations; it was based on expert advice from my primary supervisor and was inspired by transitions in game compositions.

After selecting the appropriate canonic elements, I exported the score from Finale in PDF format. I then arranged for musicians to workshop and rehearse the score. After multiple rehearsals and workshop sessions, I recorded the mezzo-soprano, tenor, and pianist in the Nickson Room at the University of Queensland School of Music. I made a professional recording in a concert hall

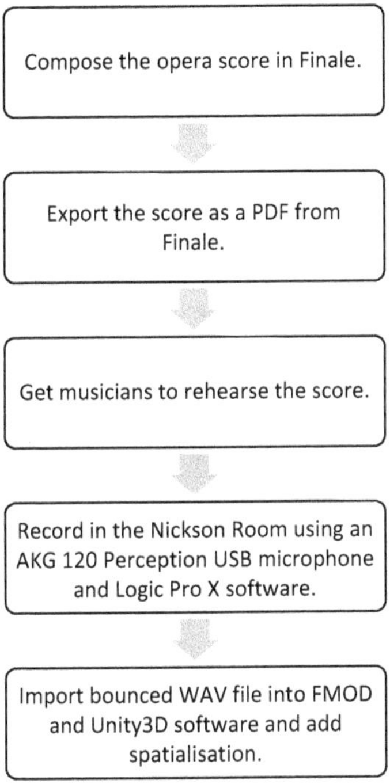

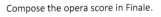

```
┌─────────────────────────────────────┐
│ Compose the opera score in Finale.  │
└─────────────────────────────────────┘
                  ▼
┌─────────────────────────────────────┐
│    Export the score as a PDF from   │
│               Finale.               │
└─────────────────────────────────────┘
                  ▼
┌─────────────────────────────────────┐
│  Get musicians to rehearse the score.│
└─────────────────────────────────────┘
                  ▼
┌─────────────────────────────────────┐
│   Record in the Nickson Room using an│
│   AKG 120 Perception USB microphone │
│       and Logic Pro X software.     │
└─────────────────────────────────────┘
                  ▼
┌─────────────────────────────────────┐
│  Import bounced WAV file into FMOD  │
│   and Unity3D software and add      │
│            spatialisation.          │
└─────────────────────────────────────┘
```

Figure 6.3 Process of music prototyping for XR.

oriented to chamber music. This condenser microphone setup picked up the acoustics of the Nickson Room realistically.

Figure 6.4 outlines the audio post-production process concerning foley and sample instruments. I experimented with combining sound recordings and mapping them to objects in Unity3D. Similarly, I experimented with synth line prototyping.

I recorded natural sounds and mapped them to virtual objects. For example, I mapped the cuckoo bird recording to the orange tree asset, which I imported from Tilt Brush Poly and recoloured in Unity3D. I combined the audio elements with the visual elements to create the theme. For instance, I used the cuckoo recording and applied spatialisation to create the impression of a bird sitting in the tree.

I experimented with synth prototyping using different Absynth and Kontakt sample instruments playing the synth line in Finale. I listened to how each sounded with the mezzo-soprano, tenor, and piano recording to select the instrument that best complemented the acoustic instruments. For the synth line timbre, I was inspired by the Blade Runner (1982) soundtrack by Vangelis (1994). I combined the synth audio file with the mezzo-soprano, tenor,

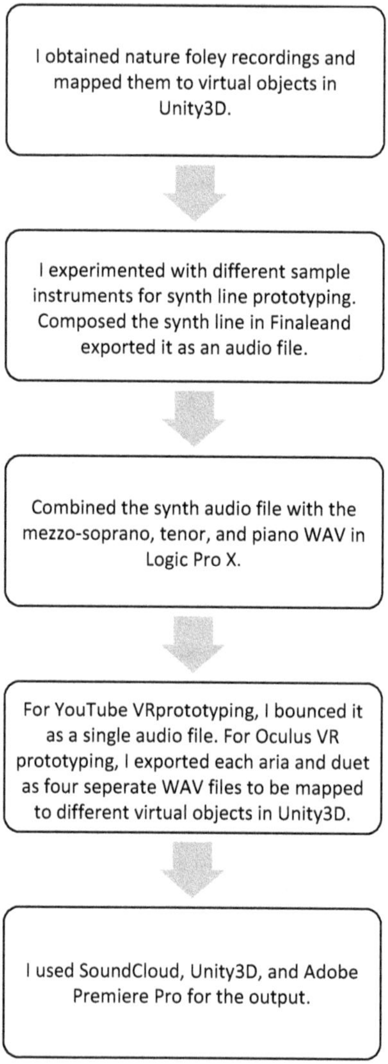

```
┌─────────────────────────────────┐
│ I obtained nature foley         │
│ recordings and mapped them to   │
│ virtual objects in Unity3D.     │
└─────────────────────────────────┘
                ↓
┌─────────────────────────────────┐
│ I experimented with different   │
│ sample instruments for synth    │
│ line prototyping. Composed the  │
│ synth line in Finale and        │
│ exported it as an audio file.   │
└─────────────────────────────────┘
                ↓
┌─────────────────────────────────┐
│ Combined the synth audio file   │
│ with the mezzo-soprano, tenor,  │
│ and piano WAV in Logic Pro X.   │
└─────────────────────────────────┘
                ↓
┌─────────────────────────────────┐
│ For YouTube VR prototyping, I   │
│ bounced it as a single audio    │
│ file. For Oculus VR             │
│ prototyping, I exported each    │
│ aria and duet as four seperate  │
│ WAV files to be mapped to       │
│ different virtual objects in    │
│ Unity3D.                        │
└─────────────────────────────────┘
                ↓
┌─────────────────────────────────┐
│ I used SoundCloud, Unity3D, and │
│ Adobe Premiere Pro for the      │
│ output.                         │
└─────────────────────────────────┘
```

Figure 6.4 Process of audio post-production for XR.

and piano WAV in Logic Pro X. I bounced this session as a single audio file for YouTube VR prototyping. I split the audio file into four parts for the Oculus VR prototyping to map each aria and duet to a different virtual asset in Unity3D. I produced the outputs using SoundCloud (for radio airplay), Unity3D for Oculus VR prototyping, and Adobe Premiere Pro for YouTube VR

Prototyping an Iterative Process 65

Figure 6.5 Process of prototyping for Oculus VR.

prototyping. The takeaway for other artists is conducting a lot of experimentation, prototyping and reflecting upon their practice.

Figure 6.5 outlines the process of prototyping for Oculus VR. First, I tested hand tracking in Unity3D and imported assets from the Unity3D store. Second, I mapped the audio files to the assets using the audio spatialiser tool and used problem statements (see Table 6.1). Third, I prototyped by adding different assets and addressing problem statements. Fourth, I tested the room size of the 'build' by walking around the virtual environment using the VR headset. I conducted paper prototyping through cyclic iterative processes. I then created and imported the Tilt Brush Poly library assets and painted the cursive text announcing the arias and duets in Tilt Brush. The final output was a build in my Oculus app; future work could be uploading it to SteamVR.

Figure 6.6 outlines the process of prototyping for YouTube VR. First, I conducted paper prototyping. I wrote down challenges and goals as bullet points. I then painted the virtual environments with Tilt Brush. I recorded the film paths in Tilt Brush and used the 360 MetaData tool to convert the Tilt Brush recording to a stereoscopic video. Subsequently, I reflected on the technological steps employed. I imported the 360° video into Adobe Premiere Pro and combined the music and film files. I then exported the VR film from Adobe Premiere Pro. Finally, I uploaded the file to YouTube.

Figure 6.7 outlines the process of prototyping for AR and visualises the macro-relationships between each prototyping stage. First, I downloaded the EyeJack Creator desktop and the EyeJack smartphone apps for prototyping. Second, I painted the AR overlay artwork with Tilt Brush. Third, I exported a snapshot and GIF of the artwork from Tilt Brush to my computer and then imported them to the EyeJack Creator application. I printed out the snapshot as the target image on A4 paper. I then placed the image on a table and scanned it with the EyeJack smartphone app. I then asked myself how it felt and looked when I scanned the image on a surface. I then tested the experience in the live opera performance setting by placing the printed image on a music stand in front of the performers and scanning it whilst they were performing.

As shown in Figure 6.8, there were overlaps in the making process. The music score was the same in all three XR experiences. Assets from Tilt Brush were used in the Oculus VR experience. The EyeJack art asset creation in Tilt Brush overlapped the AR, Oculus, and YouTube VR experience prototyping. This diagram thus shows that, although the different mediums required different software processes, there were overlaps in creating the three experiences.

6.2 Conclusion

I developed the figures in this chapter to articulate my processes and workflows to answer research question 1, 'How can self-experiential prototyping methodologies be used to create new opera experiences?'. They revealed

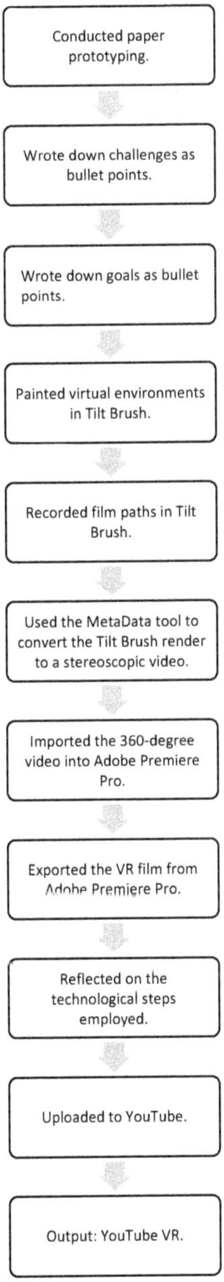

Prototyping an Iterative Process 67

```
Conducted paper prototyping.
      ↓
Wrote down challenges as bullet points.
      ↓
Wrote down goals as bullet points.
      ↓
Painted virtual environments in Tilt Brush.
      ↓
Recorded film paths in Tilt Brush.
      ↓
Used the MetaData tool to convert the Tilt Brush render to a stereoscopic video.
      ↓
Imported the 360-degree video into Adobe Premiere Pro.
      ↓
Exported the VR film from Adobe Premiere Pro.
      ↓
Reflected on the technological steps employed.
      ↓
Uploaded to YouTube.
      ↓
Output: YouTube VR.
```

Figure 6.6 Process of prototyping for YouTube VR.

68 *Creating Opera Utilising Augmented Reality*

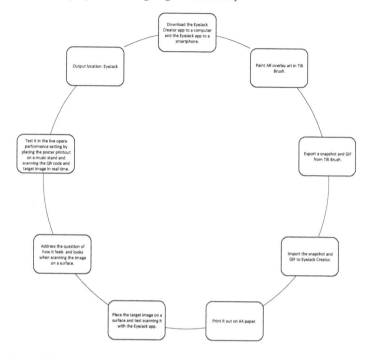

Figure 6.7 Process of prototyping for AR.

overlapping concerns in the creative process of AR, video VR, and interactive VR prototyping. I found this process enlightening as this was the first time I had examined my creative-making processes as having interconnected concerns. Research question 1 'How can self-experiential prototyping methodologies be used to create new opera experiences?' and research question 2 'What can be learnt by comparing three AR and VR opera creation processes based on the same operatic source material?' were also shown in a visual comparison through the findings in Figure 6.8 and the key interconnection that the same software can be used to create various versions of XR opera; new digital opera set creation techniques emerged from this (see Figure 6.8). I envisioned a new version of opera through the exploration of research question 1 'How can self-experiential prototyping methodologies be used to create new opera experiences?' and research question 2 'What can be learnt by comparing three AR and VR opera creation processes based on the same operatic source material?', and other practitioners may find the findings from the prototyping processes helpful in conceiving their digital opera creations. The key points and findings were that I created the best version of my work through prototyping and I hope that it offers a better user experience than previous versions. The

Prototyping an Iterative Process 69

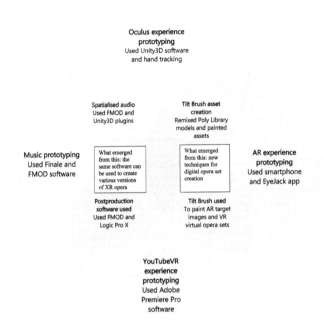

Figure 6.8 Venn diagram showing the overlaps in the creation process.

relevance of these findings for future research and practice includes the fact that my models and frameworks can be used by XR opera creators who follow in my footsteps. In Chapter 7, I present the conclusions drawn through the lens of a composer as a maker.

7 The Composer, as Maker

In this research project, I compared the iterative processes of creating an XR opera using various technological mediums; this was done to answer research question 1 'How can self-experiential prototyping methodologies be used to create new opera experiences?' and research question 2 'What can be learnt by comparing three AR and VR opera creation processes based on the same operatic source material?'. The procedures (see the figures in Chapter 6) highlighted the unique prototyping in making the opera's Oculus VR, AR, and 360° YouTube VR versions. I used a Venn diagram (see Figure 6.8) to understand and compare the connections between these processes by visualising the overlaps between the three XR productions. I hope to offer other opera creator's valuable insights into XR development by highlighting the similarities and differences between the three XR versions. The findings from research question 1 'How can self-experiential prototyping methodologies be used to create new opera experiences?' resulted in step-by-step processes of brainstorming, self-experiential prototyping, writing down problem statements, and seeking expert advice and can help other composer-makers bring their imaginations to life. This multifaceted creative process has been valuable to me, helping me to grow as a composer and become a maker of XR productions by assuming the roles of developer, designer, composer, and director.

By addressing research question 2, 'What can be learnt by comparing three AR and VR opera creation processes based on the same operatic source material?' I investigated the relationship between opera and XR from a maker's perspective, considering that opera and XR can be intricately interwoven. I discovered that audio-visual elements are in a constant interplay and that to realise the full potential of an XR production, the music and visuals must have a symbiotic relationship constructed through cyclic testing.

I found that each musical element influenced all technological elements, as the word-painting of the libretto and the musical key needed to work intrinsically to create each cohesive season of Artemis's life story. As the 360° YouTube VR version is a 20-minute VR experience, I added visual colour changes to keep the experience engaging. After exporting the 360° YouTube VR film to Adobe Premiere Pro, I thought about how I could shift the viewer's focus

DOI: 10.4324/9781003642541-7

during the experience. I did this by using the same visual environment for the entirety of the 360° YouTube VR version, changing the audience's focus using the same six-minute recording from Tilt Brush (Google, 2022), shifting focus, and applying colour changes. My methodology differs from filmmaking, which uses humans as the subjects of the frame. Film re-colourisation is used in traditional filmmaking to highlight flashbacks (see, for instance, the re-colourisation to black and white in *S4:E1 "Touch-and-Go"*, Rake, 2022), which is similar to using colour changes to shift the focus in the 360° YouTube VR version. This process enhanced the operatic content and changed my perspective as a composer, as I was required to think visually rather than merely musically. I became a composer as maker, the next section delves further into this concept.

7.1 The Producer as Composer Versus the Composer as Maker

Moorefield (2005) argues that technological advancements enable an 'all-in-one figure, a sort of apotheosis of the producer as composer' (p. xvii). According to Moorefield (2005), the producer as a composer can be likened to an auteur (director) – this book positions composers as makers. Moorefield's (2005) premise can be likened to the modern-day auteur as an XR creator. The increasingly inexpensive XR equipment (Coburn, Freeman, & Salmon, 2017) leads to the democratisation of XR, allowing a composer-maker to create XR music experiences as a one-[wo]man band.

Further, Moorefield (2005) quotes that there is no separation in what producers do in regard to them being multidisciplinary, which is comparable to the XR opera composer-maker as the embodiment of a set designer, director, librettist, and composer. Opera creation and XR creation are like composing and producing music. Composers as makers are not about 'organising and optimising the performance of others' (Moorefield, 2005, p. 55). Instead, they are the artists themselves. Moreover, the virtual worlds and the music spatialisation I created are similar to the new sonic world 'pseudo-reality, created in synthetic space' (Moorefield, 2005, p. xv) when the producer as a composer becomes a new kind of auteur. Similarly, a composer-maker of XR, especially VR, experiences can be likened to an auteur due to their multidisciplinary skills of directing, developing, and composing new interactive experiences. An example is the audio spatialisation I created in Unity3D and used in the Oculus VR version of *Artemis*, which directs the interactive audio experience.

I became an auteur of XR development and experience design auteur and created new models of opera creation. My self-experiential prototyping models can enable independent XR opera creators to explore prototyping methods and strategies for opera simulations. By creating three different versions of my opera – namely, the 360° *YouTube VR* version, the AR version, and the Oculus VR version – through self-experiential prototyping, I developed novel ways of creating each version's composition and immersive environments. The new extended space afforded by these three versions offered me a new way of viewing myself as a technologist and composer. The next section relates to research question 2, 'What can be learnt by comparing three AR and VR opera creation processes based on the same operatic source material?', as I compare the processes of AR and VR opera creation.

7.2 Three Processes of AR and VR Opera Creation

Developing opera and XR required similar creation models to create experiences that reached the hyperreality state; Clément (1988) has stated that opera is hyperreal. Both opera and XR transport audiences to another time or place through visual environments (physical or virtual). As my narrative was based on my reinterpretation of the myth of Artemis and all three versions relied heavily on my perspective, I applied a perspectivist approach, which refers to viewing the whole setting as one form of communication (Meadows, 2003) to all three versions of the work. The perspectivist approach can be likened to immersive theatre and first-person XR experiences, in which the participant is not merely a spectator. In evaluating the VR versions, a limitation of the Oculus and YouTube VR version approaches was that no character was performing. A gamified character singing the role of Artemis may have enhanced the narrative experience. According to Meadows (2003), the presence of characters in a scene increases the success of a narrative. Future XR opera creators can draw upon Dolan Paret's Framework for VR Storytelling (Bye, 2016) by substituting their experience design elements into the relevant places in the quadrants in Table 7.1. The Dolan Paret's Framework can be applied in XR opera creation for structuring work and deciding upon the impact on the story and the character presence elements for narrative design and interactivity design.

Table 7.1 Dolan Paret's Framework for VR Storytelling

Impact on Story	Character Presence	
No impact	Ghost. Ghost without impact. Observant passive. 360° videos fall into this category.	Character. Character without impact. Participant passive. First-person narrative. Sundance films fall into this category.
Impact	Ghost with impact. Observant active. *Sleep No More* falls into this category.	Character with impact. Participant active. Most agency. Façade and Grand Theft Auto fall into this category.

The next idea being argued is that the medium influenced the experience, as AR and VR influenced the experience; thus, the use of objects influenced the opera creation process. The interaction was strong in the AR version for a social audience experience and due to the scanning of the AR art. The interaction was second strongest in the Oculus VR version due to the proximity elements; the YouTube VR version was the least strong of the three due to the experience being pre-recorded. The interaction influenced the music in the Oculus VR version, as it changed the playback of the aria and duets order, making it a non-linear opera narrative; however, the music was through-composed, so the interaction did not change the structure of each composition. The narrative between the interaction and composition is thus the story season order of the musical compositions. A limitation may be that the YouTube VR narrative is not as clear as the live AR and Oculus VR versions, as it is a passive immersive experience without live singers or interactive virtual objects. The next section delves further into future work of all three versions of *Artemis*.

7.3 Future Work

The AR work was more object-oriented during onboarding, while the Oculus VR work was more technology-oriented from the outset. In my final AR prototype version at BLOOM Festival 2022, onboarding objects were available on the reception table (see media example 05). In future exhibitions and performances of the *Artemis* AR version, the onboarding objects could be handed out by the tenor as the tenor dies in the 'Winter Duet' and is left doing very little for the rest of the performance, with the QR code on one side of the object and the AR target image on the other. This distribution of the AR objects by the tenor singer can make the experience more active. The tenor can hand out seasonal paper cut-outs corresponding to each aria and duet. The audience members will be at the centre of the performance space, with the performers in a circle around them, and there will be no chairs in the venue. This setup will help the audience be drawn into the experience physically. Punchdrunk used this, with actors drawing the audience into the experience through touch and interaction. The creators of *Maya* also used this strategy. I developed these ideas by evaluating the 22 October 2022 AR performance prototype. Future performances will also be inspired by the onboarding mask objects used by Punchdrunk to immerse audiences and allow them to become part of the performances. Future performances of the AR version will be more interactive, with the singer physically leading the audience members to the performance hall as part of the onboarding experience. This change in delivery is intended to smooth the transition to the live AR experience, thereby increasing the audience's feeling of immersion in the AR performance.

In comparison to the AR version, future iterations of the Oculus VR version could have additional game discovery sounds, grabbable objects, and gamified characters to make the experience more interactive. The Oculus version is not a live performance or even necessarily a social event; what is stated here refers to exhibitions. Moreover, future iterations will draw upon the onboarding techniques of immersive theatre. Objects can turn *Artemis* into a multisensory experience in the vein of immersive theatre. Audience members will be asked to choose an object (a dried autumn leaf, a paper snowflake, a red flower, or a moon cut-out). These onboarding aspects will shape the audience members' experiences by drawing them into the virtual world of ancient Greece and will add a tangible element to the virtual experience. These onboarding and offboarding elements will be based on Punchdrunk's *Sleep No More*, in which an actor led the audience members to a bar, where they could dance with the cast members as an offboarding activity. As part of the offboarding experience, the audience kept their masks, which acted as souvenirs of the unreal world they experienced. Similarly, in *Artemis*, spectators will keep their onboarding cut-outs as mementos of the magical experience of travelling to ancient Greece and hearing the myth of Artemis. The onboarding objects will induce time travel into *Artemis*, inspired by Mary Hoffman's non-linear novel *Stravaganza*, in which the main character has a talisman that enables time travelling to ancient Italy. Based on expert feedback that I received from Gameloft mentors at the GameOn Festival 2022, the next step for the Oculus VR version will be to link the objects to sound files. When an audience member picks up a physical object, the foley of that object will be heard, while the virtual objects connected to the arias and duets will still be vases. Following the techniques used in *SOMNAI: Lucid dreaming*, physical vases and temple objects with narrative functions can be used. This combination of physical objects and sound files can increase immersion. Moreover, a specific object can be assigned to each audience member, just as each is assigned a seat in a traditional opera venue. According to design and cognition theorists, the affordances of objects are highly important (Worthen, 2012, p. 96) for conveying a story and adding to the overall immersive experience of a production.

Composing for VR and AR mediums entails media-based immersion by making set designs similar to film sets or immersive theatre. In future exhibitions of the Oculus VR *Artemis* version, additional staging elements will include dry leaves placed in the space. These tactile elements will be incorporated to immerse the audience in the experience whilst listening to the 'Autumn Ayre' aria. In the spring environment of 'Licht und Liebe', rose water can be sprayed to provide an olfactory experience. In the summer environment of 'Mi amor la luna', a fan blowing warm air can be placed in front of the participants to create the immersive experience of being in a hot summer environment. In 'Winter Duet', confetti will be dropped onto the participants to create the tactile experience of falling snow. As an offboarding activity, audience members may take home any of these objects alongside their onboarding cut-out object. I realised the importance of including a gamified performer through the comparative process. I realised this through expert advice from my primary supervisor. Including a gamified character in the Oculus VR and YouTube VR versions could make them as engaging as the AR version, as characters increase the effectiveness of a narrative. According to Meadows (2003), characters give the narrative soul. The next section will delve further into my journey.

7.4 My Journey

By exploring the two research questions, this work has transformed me into a multidisciplinary composer, technologist, social media presence, extended reality developer, game sound implementor, and founder of the start-up TechOperaXR. Where I want to go from here is creating more extended reality music experiences and artworks to increase the prevalence of stories that feature diverse stories. I also plan to continue my start-up journey and create international productions for large and independent opera companies. I want to create extended reality works for multi-genre festivals, museums, and art galleries. The story of Artemis will stay with me forever. As a role model for strong women and a protectress of young girls and nature, she embodies multiple psychological archetypes that resonate with me. I became an XR developer, self-experiential tester, solo creator, and composer-maker during my Artemis journey. Throughout this project, Artemis guided me in becoming a multifaceted composer and digital work creator.

The journey of a book changes the writer, just as a successful XR experience changes the audience. The journey shapes the creator and the experiencer through many transitions, like the waxing and waning of the moon. As the goddess of transitions, Artemis inspired me to transition from the role of a music technologist and composer to the role of a composer maker through my journey in this project. My work as a composer-maker can help the next generation of makers, just as Artemis helped the next generation of girls. By delving into research question 1 'How can self-experiential prototyping methodologies be used to create new opera experiences?', self-experiential prototyping resulted in the creation of the new tech-opera *Artemis*, and the comparison of the innovative techniques employed to explore research question 2 'What can be learnt by comparing three AR and VR opera creation processes based on the same operatic source material?' resulted in a new methodology for opera creation for future creators.

Appendix 1 – Media Appendix

Experience 1: BLOOM Illuminate Light and Sound Display

Media example 01:

http://taanarosemusic.weebly.com/phd-portfolio-bloom.html/#Media-example-01

Media example 02:

http://taanarosemusic.weebly.com/phd-portfolio-bloom.html/#Media-example-02

Media example 03:

http://taanarosemusic.weebly.com/phd-portfolio-bloom.html/#Media-example-03

Media example 04:

http://taanarosemusic.weebly.com/phd-portfolio-bloom.html/#Media-example-04

Experience 2: Artemis XR Opera

Media example 05:

http://taanarosemusic.weebly.com/phd-portfolio-artemis-xr-opera.html#Media-example-05

Media example 06:

http://taanarosemusic.weebly.com/phd-portfolio-artemis-xr-opera.html#Media-example-06

Media example 07:

http://taanarosemusic.weebly.com/phd-portfolio-artemis-xr-opera.html#Media-example-07

Media example 08:

http://taanarosemusic.weebly.com/phd-portfolio-artemis-xr-opera.html#Media-example-08

Media example 09:

http://taanarosemusic.weebly.com/phd-portfolio-artemis-xr-opera.html#Media-example-09

Media example 10:

http://taanarosemusic.weebly.com/phd-portfolio-artemis-xr-opera.html#Media-example-10

Media example 11:

http://taanarosemusic.weebly.com/phd-portfolio-artemis-xr-opera.html#Media-example-11

Experience 3: Artemis YouTubeVR

Media example 12:

http://taanarosemusic.weebly.com/phd-portfolio-artemis-vr-youtubevr.html#Media-example-12

Media example 13:

http://taanarosemusic.weebly.com/phd-portfolio-artemis-vr-youtubevr.html#Media-example-13

Appendix 1 – Media Appendix 79

Media example 14:

http://taanarosemusic.weebly.com/phd-portfolio-artemis-vr-youtubevr.html#Media-example-14

Media example 15:

http://taanarosemusic.weebly.com/phd-portfolio-artemis-vr-youtubevr.html#Media-example-15

Media example 16:

http://taanarosemusic.weebly.com/phd-portfolio-artemis-vr-youtubevr.html#Media-example-16

Media example 17:

http://taanarosemusic.weebly.com/phd-portfolio-artemis-vr-youtubevr.html#Media-example-17

Media example 18:

http://taanarosemusic.weebly.com/phd-portfolio-artemis-vr-youtubevr.html#Media-example-18

Experience 4: Artemis Oculus VR

Media example 19:

http://taanarosemusic.weebly.com/phd-portfolio-artemis-oculus-vr.html#Media-example-19

Media example 20:

http://taanarosemusic.weebly.com/phd-portfolio-artemis-oculus-vr.html#Media-example-20

Media example 21:

http://taanarosemusic.weebly.com/phd-portfolio-artemis-oculus-vr.html#Media-example-21

Appendix 1 – Media Appendix

Media example 22:

http://taanarosemusic.weebly.com/phd-portfolio-artemis-oculus-vr.html#Media-example-22

Media example 23:

http://taanarosemusic.weebly.com/phd-portfolio-artemis-oculus-vr.html#Media-example-23

Media example 24:

http://taanarosemusic.weebly.com/phd-portfolio-artemis-oculus-vr.html#Media-example-24

Media example 25:

http://taanarosemusic.weebly.com/phd-portfolio-artemis-oculus-vr.html#Media-example-25

Media example 26:

http://taanarosemusic.weebly.com/phd-portfolio-artemis-oculus-vr.html#Media-example-26

Media example 27:

http://taanarosemusic.weebly.com/phd-portfolio-artemis-oculus-vr.html#Media-example-27

Media example 28:

http://taanarosemusic.weebly.com/phd-portfolio-artemis-oculus-vr.html#Media-example-28

Media example 29:

http://taanarosemusic.weebly.com/phd-portfolio-artemis-oculus-vr.html#Media-example-29

Appendix 1 – Media Appendix 81

PHD Portfolio Walkthrough Videos

Media example 30:

http://taanarosemusic.weebly.com/phd-portfolio-walkthrough-videos.html#Media-example-30

Media example 31:

http://taanarosemusic.weebly.com/phd-portfolio-walkthrough-videos.html#Media-example-31

Media example 32:

http://taanarosemusic.weebly.com/phd-portfolio-walkthrough-videos.html#Media-example-32

Artemis Score

Media example 33:

http://taanarosemusic.weebly.com/artemis-score.html#Media-example-33

Media example 34:

http://taanarosemusic.weebly.com/artemis-score.html#Media-example-34

More Arrangements and Compositions

Media example 35:

http://taanarosemusic.weebly.com/phd-portfolio-more-arrangements-and-compositions.html#Media-example-35

Media example 36:

http://taanarosemusic.weebly.com/phd-portfolio-more-arrangements-and-compositions.html#Media-example-36

82 *Appendix 1 – Media Appendix*

Media example 37:

http://taanarosemusic.weebly.com/phd-portfolio-more-arrangements-and-compositions.html#Media-example-37

Media example 38:

http://taanarosemusic.weebly.com/phd-portfolio-more-arrangements-and-compositions.html#Media-example-38

Media example 39:

http://taanarosemusic.weebly.com/phd-portfolio-more-arrangements-and-compositions.html#Media-example-39

Media example 40:

http://taanarosemusic.weebly.com/phd-portfolio-more-arrangements-and-compositions.html#Media-example-40

Media example 41:

http://taanarosemusic.weebly.com/phd-portfolio-more-arrangements-and-compositions.html#Media-example-41

Media example 42:

http://taanarosemusic.weebly.com/phd-portfolio-more-arrangements-and-compositions.html#Media-example-42

Media example 43:

http://taanarosemusic.weebly.com/phd-portfolio-more-arrangements-and-compositions.html#Media-example-43

Media example 44:

http://taanarosemusic.weebly.com/phd-portfolio-more-arrangements-and-compositions.html#Media-example-44

Media example 45:

http://taanarosemusic.weebly.com/phd-portfolio-more-arrangements-and-compositions.html#Media-example-45

Media example 46:

http://taanarosemusic.weebly.com/phd-portfolio-more-arrangements-and-compositions.html#Media-example-46

Media example 47:

http://taanarosemusic.weebly.com/phd-portfolio-more-arrangements-and-compositions.html#Media-example-47

Media example 48:

http://taanarosemusic.weebly.com/phd-portfolio-more-arrangements-and-compositions.html#Media-example-48

Media example 49:

http://taanarosemusic.weebly.com/phd-portfolio-more-arrangements-and-compositions.html#Media-example-49

Media example 50:

http://taanarosemusic.weebly.com/phd-portfolio-more-arrangements-and-compositions.html#Media-example-50

Media example 51:

http://taanarosemusic.weebly.com/phd-portfolio-more-arrangements-and-compositions.html#Media-example-51

Media example 52:

http://taanarosemusic.weebly.com/phd-portfolio-more-arrangements-and-compositions.html#Media-example-52

84   Appendix 1 – Media Appendix

Media example 53:

http://taanarosemusic.weebly.com/phd-portfolio-more-arrangements-and-compositions.html#Media-example-53

Media example 54:

http://taanarosemusic.weebly.com/phd-portfolio-more-arrangements-and-compositions.html#Media-example-54

Media example 55:

http://taanarosemusic.weebly.com/phd-portfolio-more-arrangements-and-compositions.html#Media-example-55

Media example 56:

http://taanarosemusic.weebly.com/phd-portfolio-more-arrangements-and-compositions.html#Media-example-56

Media example 57:

http://taanarosemusic.weebly.com/phd-portfolio-more-arrangements-and-compositions.html#Media-example-57

Media example 58:

http://taanarosemusic.weebly.com/phd-portfolio-more-arrangements-and-compositions.html#Media-example-58

Media example 59:

http://taanarosemusic.weebly.com/phd-portfolio-more-arrangements-and-compositions.html#Media-example-59

Appendix 2 – Librettos

Artemis

Librettist and Translator: Taana Rose

Translation of the Libretto

I wish you light and love
And to all, all, yes, all people.
Yes I wish you, light and love. Yes!
Love, love, I wish you, everything comes at the right time.
Trust the future. Love, o, your love is as red as the flowers in the field.
Love, o, love, as red as the flowers in the field.
Heavens, full of stars, we are all stars.
Millions of stars.
The stars sparkle like lights over the world.
Music is the love, like the stars in the sky, reliable, star clear night, splendour.
The child laughs and does what it wants.
Music is the love.
Music is the love.
Music is the love.
Music is the love.
Music is the love.
Light and love, to all people, love, love, I wish you love, light and love.

Light and love.
I wish you light.
Leaves are turning hearts burning.
Autumn as colourful as spring with leaves instead of poppies, red leaves like my love for the forest, yes!
My fellow deer and nymphs.
Love oh love for this natural world, I am the goddess of this forest.

Zeus and Leto brought me to protect our forests and our daughters, all.
Millions of stars light my way.
The stars dance in their heavenly velvet blanket above the world.
I declare that I will kill every animal in the world as I love to hunt.
Gaia is angry, she has sent a scorpion to kill thee Orion.
Stars dance.
Orion my love.
Artemis my love.
You are lost. I am the goddess of the hunt. The scorpion has arrived.
Gaia has taken me.
I render thee in the stars.

Leaves are turning hearts burning, burning.
The cold creeps in gives you pins and needles.
Dusk turns to dawn, you are reborn, you are reborn.
Once forlorn you are reborn, you are reborn.
Winter has come, do not feel numb, you are full of life, you got through your strife.
Ah ah ah.
Come, do not feel numb, you are full of life, you got through your strife.
Ah ah ah.

Leaves are turning hearts are burning, burning.
The cold crept in gave me pins and needles, I survived the hunt.
At dawn, the forest is reborn, reborn.
Once forlorn you are reborn, you are reborn.
Winter has come, do not feel numb, you are full of life, you got through your strife.

My love, the moon.
The moon, my love.
My love, the moon, the moon, my love.
The moon, my love.
My love, the moon, the moon, my love.
I love the moon, she sees me through the darkest nights and reignites, all of the lights.
The moon, my love.
The moon, my love.
My love, the moon, the moon my love.
My love, the moon.
The moon my love.
My love, the moon, the moon, my love.

All of the lights, come back on, you are feeling strong.
I love the moon she sees me through.
The darkest nights, and reignites, all of the lights.
My love, the moon.
The moon, my love.
My love, the moon.
The moon, my love.

Appendix 3 – Scores

Artemis XR Opera

Media example 33:

http://taanarosemusic.weebly.com/artemis-score.html#Media-example-33

Media example 34:

http://taanarosemusic.weebly.com/artemis-score.html#Media-example-34

References

A Vixens Tale. (2019). Welsh National Opera. [Augmented reality tunnel]. Wales Millennium Centre, Wales.

Abbate, C., & Parker, R. (2012). *A history of opera: The last four hundred years*. London, England: Penguin UK.

AIR-EDEL MUSIC. (2019, July 29). Scoring and Songwriting 'Astrologaster' for Nyamyam Games [Web log post]. Retrieved from https://airedelcouk.wordpress.com/2019/07/29/scoring-and-songwriting-astrologaster-for-nyamyam-games/

Albert-Puleo, Michael. (1978). Mythobotany, pharacology, and chemistry of thujone-containing plants and derivatives. *Economic Botany, 32*(1), 65–74. https://link.springer.com/article/10.1007/BF02906731

Aronson, A. (1999). Technology and dramaturgical development: Five observations. *Theatre Research International, 24*(2), 188–197. Retrieved from https://doi.org/10.1017/S0307883300020812

Auslander, P. (1999). *Liveness: Performance in a mediatized culture*. London, England: Routledge.

Australian Government. (2016). National Opera Review. Retrieved from https://www.arts.gov.au/sites/default/files/documents/national_opera_review_final_report_0.pdf

Aylett, R., & Louchart, S. (2007). Being there: Participants and spectators in interactive narrative. In M. Cavazza & S. Donikian (Eds), *Virtual storytelling. Using virtual reality technologies for storytelling. ICVS 2007.* Lecture Notes in Computer Science, vol 4871. Berlin, Germany: Springer. Retrieved from https://doi.org/10.1007/978-3-540-77039-8_10

Bailenson, J. (2018). *Experience on demand: What virtual reality is, how it works, and what it can do*. New York City, NY: WW Norton & Company.

Barrett, F., & Doyle, M. (Directors). (2003). *Sleep no more*. [Live immersive theatre performance] The McKittrick Hotel, New York City. Punchdrunk.

Barrett, F., & Doyle, M. (Directors). (2005). *The firebird ball*. [Live immersive theatre performance] Offley Works, London. Punchdrunk.

Barrett, F., & Doyle, M. (Directors). (2006). *Faust*. [Live immersive theatre performance] Wapping Lane, London. Punchdrunk.

Beacham, R. C. (1994). *Adolphe Appia: Artist and visionary of the modern theatre*. Philadelphia, PA: Harwood Academic Publishers.

Belbase, S., Luitel, B., & Taylor, P. (2008). Autoethnography: A method of research and teaching for transformative education. *Journal of Education and Research, 1*(1), 86–95. Retrieved from https://eric.ed.gov/?id=ED501840

References

Benford, S., & Giannachi, G. (2011). *Performing mixed reality*. Cambridge, MA: MIT Press.

Benford, S., & Giannachi, G. (2012). Interaction as performance. *Interactions (New York, N.Y.), 19*(3), 38–43. Retrieved from https://doi.org/10.1145/2168931.2168941

Benyon, D. (2013). *Designing Interactive Systems PDF ETextbook*. Harlow, England: Pearson Education, Limited. Retrieved from https://pubhtml5.com/huyw/zjih/Designing_Interactive_Systems_A_Comprehensive_Guide_to_HCI%2C_UX_and_Interaction_Design_PDFDrive_/

Biggin, R. (2017). *Immersive theatre and audience experience*. Basingstoke, England: Palgrave Macmillan.

Blackwood, S., Lim, L., Polias, P., & Van Reyk, B. (2019). Opera and the Doing of Women. Arts Hub. Retrieved from https://performing.artshub.com.au/news-article/opinions-and-analysis/performing-arts/blackwood-lim-polias-and-van-reyk/opera-and-the-doing-of-women-257968

Bolen, J. S. (2014). *Artemis: The indomitable spirit in everywoman*. Newburyport, MA: Conari Press.

Bolter, J. D., & Grusin, R. A. (1996). Remediation. *Configurations, 4*(3), 311–358. https://doi.org/10.1353/con.1996.0018

Botsman, T. (2020). Reimagining the Dinosaur: Opera After COVID-19 [Web log post]. Artshub, Retrieved from https://www.artshub.com.au/news/opinions-analysis/reimagining-the-dinosaur-opera-after-covid-19-260069-2366827/

Brown, Y. (n.d.). About Audio Middleware [Web log post] Yannis Brown - Game Audio Specialist. Retrieved from https://www.yannisbrown.com/about-audio-middleware/#:~:text=Audio%20middleware%20is%20a%20third,from%20a%20set%20of%20sounds

Bucher, J. (2018). *Storytelling for virtual reality* (1st ed.). Oxford, England: Routledge.

Budin, S. L. (2015). *Artemis*. Oxfordshire, England: Routledge.

Bye, K. (Producer). (2016). *Voices of VR* [Audio podcast]. Retrieved from https://voicesofvr.com/292-the-four-different-types-of-stories-in-vr/

Candy, L. (2006). Practice based research: A guide. *CCS Report*, 1, 1–19. Retrieved from https://d1wqtxts1xzle7.cloudfront.net/38232000/Candy_Practice_Based_Research_A_Guide-libre.pdf?1437350794=&response-content-disposition=inline%3B+filename%3DPractice_Based_Research_A_Guide.pdf&Expires=1677134738&Signature=P9LqYQ6-S39DsKB1Q6OFFHDUjPJ1XAmY3x3G5lQg-Y8gAXKo83--0JvVX1q7BTm7lYa2tzjjU9tWYL2UyJ8S6wZBixugUOpVgQ9aktciEj9TrL--Kg93i987oT7wU3b~a~tqDZG6JvLBpfZHI-ABvIxsCHIfDf5mHteJKr8QC-SgFNPfk-f87X5P9wOlv8pVq6cf1jioWEgCYJD2YtwgQnTcpPlixWAEsyX8E7sSLPT028~gJavKIJAfwWNCZyaj18994r~q-wrmiTfE-6o31wPn~BaPf0mE-dL2FGNZc6nP3LbHtkPpaF2JztANIiRZ~8hu4C6RPBZrGsh6EQMwmQ__&Key-Pair-Id=APKAJLOHF5GGSLRBV4ZA

Clément, C. (1988). *Opera, or the undoing of women*. Minneapolis, MN: The University of Minnesota Press.

Coburn, J. Q., Freeman, I., & Salmon, J. L. (2017). A review of the capabilities of current low-cost virtual reality technology and its potential to enhance the design process. *Journal of Computing and Information Science in Engineering, 17*(3). https://doi.org/10.1115/1.4036921

Cockburn, P. (2022, October 6). Opera Australia Artistic Director Lyndon Terracini Latest to Walk Away from Arts Company. *ABC News*. Retrieved from https://www.abc.net.

References

au/news/2022-10-06/opera-australia-artistic-director-lyndon-terracini-quits/1015 06920

Collins, K. (2008). *Game sound: An introduction to the history, theory, and practice of video game music and sound design.* Cambridge, MA: MIT Press.

Cook, D. (1996). *The culture industry revisited: Theodor W. Adorno on mass culture.* Washington, DC: Rowman & Littlefield Publishers.

Cooper, J. C. (1978). *An illustrated encyclopaedia of symbols.* London, England: Thames and Hudson.

Creswell, J. (2002). *Educational research: Planning, conducting, and evaluating quantitative and qualitative research.* Upper Saddle River, NJ: Merrill Prentice Hall.

Crowley, A. (n.d.). *Pan to Artemis.* Retrieved from https://www.poetry.com/poem/385/pan-to-artemis

Current, Rising [Hyperreality opera performance]. Fernando (Director) (2020). London, England. Royal Opera House.

Deathridge, J. (1974). The nomenclature of Wagner's sketches. *Proceedings of the Royal Musical Association, 101*(1), 75–83. https://doi.org/10.1093/jrma/101.1.75

Doerr, A. (2014). *All the light we cannot see.* New York City, NY: Scribner.

Dziuda, Ł., Biernacki, M. P., Baran, P. M., & Truszczyński, O. E. (2014). The effects of simulated fog and motion on simulator sickness in a driving simulator and the duration of after-effects. *Applied Ergonomics, 45*(3), 406–412. Retrieved from https://doi.org/10.1016/j.apergo.2013.05.003

Eglinton, A. (2010). Reflections on a decade of Punchdrunk Theatre. *TheatreForum, 37,* 46–55. Retrieved from https://search.proquest.com/docview/633117397?accountid=14723

Eiddior, G. (Director). (2017). *Magic Butterfly* [VR performance]. Multiple locations. Welsh National Opera. Retrieved from: https://www.youtube.com/watch?v=cBW8KVRhZEs

Ellis, C., & Bochner, A. (2000). Autoethnography, personal narrative, reflexivity: Researcher as subject. In Autoethnography, Personal Narrative, Reflexivity: Researcher as Subject, N. K. Denzin & Y. S. Lincoln (Eds.), *Handbook of qualitative research* (2nd Ed., pp. 733–768). The University of South Florida: Sage Publications.

Emmerson, S. (1998). Aural landscape: Musical space. *Organised Sound: An International Journal of Music Technology, 3*(2), 135–140. Retrieved from https://doi.org/10.1017/S1355771898002064

Espinosa, A. (2007). Music: a bridge between two cultures. In *Forum on Public Policy Online* (Vol. 2007, No. 3, p. n3). Oxford Round Table. 406 West Florida Avenue, Urbana, IL 61801.

Eternal Sunshine of the Spotless Mind (2004). Michel Gondry. Focus Features, Anonymous Content, This Is That Productions.

Exploreengage (2010). Opera Australia Augmented Reality [Video file]. Retrieved from https://www.youtube.com/watch?v=qa6QvH47yoA

Fawcett-Lothson, A. (2009). The Florentine Camerata and their influence on the beginnings of opera. *IU South Bend Undergraduate Research Journal, 9,* 29–34. Retrieved from https://scholarworks.iu.edu/journals/index.php/iusburj/article/download/19724/25807/

Gluck, C. (1762). *Orpheus & Eurydice.*

Grout, D., & Williams, H. W. (2003). A short history of opera. In *A Short History of Opera* (pp. 1-575). New York City, NY: Columbia University Press.

92 References

Goethe, J. W. (1832). *Faust*. London, England: Thomas Boosey and Sons. (Original work published 1821).

Goldstone, W. (2009). *Unity game development essentials*. Birmingham, England: Packt Publishing.

Google. (2022). *Tilt Brush* [Computer software]. Retrieved from https://store.steampowered.com/app/327140/Tilt_Brush/

Grout, D., & Williams, H. W. (2003). A short history of opera. In *A short history of opera*. New York City, NY: Columbia University Press.

Guyenette, C. (Director). (2017). *SOMNAI: Lucid Dreaming*. [Virtual reality immersive production]. Dotdotdot, London, UK.

Haake, S. (2019). Stealing the exams: Using narrative techniques in designing an Escape Game in University Context. In *European Conference on Games Based Learning* (pp. 1004–XVI). Reading: Academic Conferences International Limited. Retrieved from https://www.proquest.com/openview/0d7f9e4b445a1b4c0c3f357a1e08b57a/1?cbl=396495&pq-origsite=gscholar

Handel, G. (1710). *Apollo & Daphne*.

Hamilton, R. (2019). Collaborative and competitive futures for virtual reality music and sound. In *2019 IEEE Conference on Virtual Reality and 3D User Interfaces (VR)* (pp. 1510–1512). https://doi.org/10.1109/VR.2019.8798166

Hann, R. (2012). Dwelling in light and sound: An intermedial site for digital opera. *International Journal of Performance Arts and Digital Media*, 8(1), 61–78. Retrieved from https://doi.org/10.1386/padm.8.1.61_1

Haptical. (2017, October 23). Computer Scientists Build Avatars to Experience Magic Butterfly Opera in VR. Retrieved from https://haptic.al/computer-scientists-build-avatars-to-experience-magic-butterfly-opera-in-vr-95efd98cf8b5

Hartson, R., & Pyla, P. (2012). *The UX book*. San Francisco, CA: Elsevier Science & Technology.

Hoffman, M. (2006). *Stravaganza: City of flowers*. New York, NY: Bloomsbury Publishing.

Hoffman, M. (2008a). *The Falconer's knot*. London, UK: A&C Black.

Hoffman, M. (2008b). *City of masks* (Vol. 1). London, England: A&C Black.

Hoffman, M. (2010). *City of stars*. New York, NY: Bloomsbury Children's Books.

Hoffman, M. (2012a). *Stravaganza: City of swords* (Vol. 6). London, England: A&C Black.

Hoffman, M. (2012b). *City of ships*. New York, NY: Bloomsbury Children's Books.

Howitt, P. (Director). (1998). *Sliding Doors* [Motion picture; Netflix]. United Kingdom & United States Intermedia Films, Mirage Enterprises, Miramax, Paramount Pictures.

Hudson, S., Matson-Barkat, S., Pallamin, N., & Jegou, G. (2019). With or without you? Interaction and immersion in a virtual reality experience. *Journal of Business Research*, 100, 459–468. Retrieved from https://doi.org/10.1016/j.jbusres.2018.10.062

Hughes, J. D. (1990). Goddess of conservation. *Forest and Conservation History*, 1, 191–197. Retrieved from https://www.thetempleofnature.org/_dox/artemis-goddess-of-conservation.pdf

Jaehnig, J. (2019). Tech Goes to the Opera with New AR Experience. Retrieved from https://arpost.co/2019/10/04/tech-goes-to-the-opera-with-new-ar-experience/

Javornik, A., Rogers, Y., Gander, D., & Moutinho, A. (2017). MagicFace: Stepping into character through an augmented reality mirror. In *Proceedings of the 2017 CHI*

References

Conference on Human Factors in Computing Systems (pp. 4838–4849). Retrieved from https://dl.acm.org/doi/pdf/10.1145/3025453.3025722

Josselson, R. (2010). Narrative research. In N. J. Salkind (Ed.), *Encyclopedia of research design* (pp. 869–874). Thousand Oaks, CA: Sage Publications.

Jessop, E. N., Torpey, P. A., & Bloomberg, B. (2011, May). Music and technology in death and the powers. In *NIME* (pp. 349–354). MIT Media Lab. Academia Edu. Retrieved from: https://d1wqtxts1xzle7.cloudfront.net/3498854/jessop_torpey_bloomberg_nime2011_technology_death_and_the_powers-libre.pdf?1390834023=&response-content-disposition=inline%3B+filename%3DMusic_and_Technology_in_Death_and_the_Po.pdf-&Expires=1746513810&Signature=gleIIAvzUyFWQh4UAgsmE2Xwe7J~5wiDwnPWR5HYwDVAtwTG3TDOYxbYkkvowVjYdMeswgx0A5Fx~zVB7swkrHhB9xUcG8X9clbq1DWPJL3obi0I6gvR0f53CIALAStTOwBsbpjrOCP4RHY58S6Q2ioSglqfPAb~-paWKRtSaVLVX2OF1vaKua4QjPjVKXrCtWRpZ8m0P1-c7XrDzdSUd07lN-0bqGRAsOt4G2qJH6224Esb7ae9bYY~Ht6BEtAQdBiq~Q3wBqf8jUd5I-uugvM-0fy6my3v14lW6fcRUYsVXAFumg02qVmQhv2C0RGI4Y5KilYGVCdT2Q5yzm-Bom0-w__&Key-Pair-Id=APKAJLOHF5GGSLRBV4ZA

Jung, T., tom Dieck, M. C., Lee, H., & Chung, N. (2016). Effects of virtual reality and augmented reality on visitor experiences in museum. In *Information and Communication Technologies in Tourism 2016: Proceedings of the International Conference in Bilbao, Spain, February 2–5, 2016* (pp. 621–635). Springer International Publishing. Retrieved from https://d1wqtxts1xzle7.cloudfront.net/42292467/Effects_of_Virtual_Reality_and_Augmented_Reality_on_Visitor_Experiences_in_Museum_fin-Athors_copy-libre.pdf?1454850907=&response-content-disposition=inline%3B+filename%3DEffects_of_Virtual_Reality_and_Augmented.pdf&Expires=1746513999&Signature=cwy-cUlaj~SkybIveKQ~P4jKdioh1KG6-7b6BNcsdmtuQ0t24nYYl0t5F5og7xbd-2sC0h0hlWgSjrUkaVr4hGjaScUVxoYKRmzHbrYAbz-SYMlxucjRA7lx5J1XGPBsnnCDgAg9jIRNnjspBjXrah51T7l7HPE~APeEdoutShhdhyLR-DBe37VKj2PGDhJWx~A5syBeDn4FQDHvpSXYwmpUagljAcNhhydXXko1PF-UrXO-xCvC-oxmyrSPyZqMI-wXJFSI-L7bX-zoxJdgu1S~EyhNqZ~uVoToU4uJn9vqQH21cBw0wCgFiq7OW7JKSV0snEvBrY5v-5zwlv0ctVPA__&Key-Pair-Id=APKAJLOHF5GGSLRBV4ZA

Kajastila, R., & Takala, T. (2008). Interaction in digitally augmented opera. In *Proceedings of International Conference on Digital Arts* (pp. 216–219). Retrieved from https://repositorioaberto.uab.pt/bitstream/10400.2/1973/1/ProceedingsArtech08.pdf#page=227

Kennedy, H., & Atkinson, S. (2018). Extended reality ecosystems: Innovations in creativity and collaboration in the theatrical arts. *Refractory: A Journal of Entertainment Media, 30*(10), 1-12. Retrieved from: https://nottingham-repository.worktribe.com/output/3685279/extended-reality-ecosystems-innovations-in-creativity-and-collaboration-in-the-theatrical-arts

Kerslake, B. (2002). *Contemporary opera and the role of technology* (Unpublished master's thesis). Griffith University, Brisbane, Australia.

Laurel, B. (2013). *Computers as theatre*. Boston, MA: Addison-Wesley.

Lester, N. (2018). *The Paris seamstress*. Sydney, Australia: Hachette Australia.

Lewis, C. S. (1950). *The lion, the witch and the wardrobe*. London, England: Geoffrey Bles.

Littlejohn, D. (1992). *The ultimate art: Essays around and about opera*. Berkeley, CA: The University of California Press.

References

Lucas, J., Cornish, T., & Margolis, T. (2012). To a cultural perspective of mixed reality events: A case study of event overflow in operas and concerts in mixed reality. *New Review of Hypermedia and Multimedia: Cultures in Virtual Worlds, 18*(4), 277–293. Retrieved from https://www.tandfonline.com/doi/full/10.1080/13614568.2012.746741

Luitel, B. C. (2009). Storying, critical reflexivity, and imagination. In *Contemporary qualitative research* (pp. 217–228). Dordrecht, Netherlands: Springer Netherlands. Retrieved from https://doi.org/10.1007/978-1-4020-5920-9_19

Machon, J. (Ed.). (2017). *Immersive theatres: Intimacy and immediacy in contemporary performance.* Bloomsbury, London: Bloomsbury Publishing.

Macpherson, B. (2012). Embodying the virtual: 'Digital opera' as a new Gesamtkunstwerk? *International Journal of Performance Arts & Digital Media, 8*(1), 49–60. https://doi.org/10.1386/padm.8.1.49_1

Marasco, A., Balbi, B., & Icolari, D. (2018). Augmented La Traviata: Remediating opera through augmented reality technology. *International Journal of Art, Culture and Design Technologies (IJACDT), 7*(2), 41–64. Retrieved from https://www.researchgate.net/publication/330746404_Augmented_La_Traviata_Remediating_Opera_Through_Augmented_Reality_Technology

McClanahan, R. (1999). *Word painting: A guide to writing more descriptively.* London, England: Penguin.

McClary, S. (2011). Feminine endings at twenty. *Trans. Revista Transcultural de Música, 15*, 1–10. Retrieved from https://www.redalyc.org/pdf/822/82222646002.pdf

Meadows, M. S. (2003). *Pause & effect: The art of interactive narrative.* Indianapolis, IN: New Riders.

Merriam-Webster. (n.d.). Multimodal. *Merriam-Webster.com dictionary.* Retrieved January 18, 2023, from https://www.merriam-webster.com/dictionary/multimodal

Montefiore, S. (2005). *The beekeeper's daughter.* New York, NY: Simon & Schuster.

Moorefield, V. (2005). *The producer as composer: Shaping the sounds of popular music.* Cambridge, MA: MIT Press.

Moshel, D. (Director). (2018). V-Aria [Opera]. [Bavaria, Germany]: Bayrische Staatsoper.

Murphie, A. (1997). Pierre Lévy, Qu'est-ce que le virtuel? [What is the virtual?] (Paris: Editions La Découverte, 1995), 157 pp. French language. ISBN 2 7071 2515 6; and Giulio Blasi and Andrea Bernadelli, Semiotics and the Effects-of-Media-Change Research Programmes, Versus 72, settembredicembre 1995, pp. 159. (English, French and Italian languages), ISSN 88 452 2789 8. *Convergence (London, England), 3*(2), 122–126. Retrieved from https://doi.org/10.1177/135485659700300212

Niffenegger, A. (2004). *The time traveller's wife.* San Fransisco, CA: MacAdam/Cage.

Nitschke, M. (2018). Maya

Nitschke, M. (2018a, April 9). *MAYA - Mixed-reality-techno-opera (trailer)* [Video file]. Retrieved from https://vimeo.com/263934654

Nitschke, M. (2018b, June 19). *MAYA - The app for the mixed-reality-techno-opera* [Video file]. Retrieved from https://www.youtube.com/watch?v=x6L-Me2Wuj4

Nolan, C. (Director). (2000). *Memento* [Motion picture]. United States. Newmarket Capital Group, Team Todd, I Remember Productions, Summit Entertainment.

Norman, D. A. (2013). *The design of everyday things* (Revised and expanded edition.). Cambridge, MA: MIT Press.

Number None. (2009). *Braid* [Mac OS version]. Microsoft Games Studios. Retrieved from Steam https://store.steampowered.com/app/26800/Braid/

References

Ortiz-de-Urbina, P. (Ed.). (2020). *Germanic myths in the audiovisual culture.* Tübingen, Germany: Narr Francke Attempto Verlag.

Peters, E., Heijligers, B., Kievith, J., Razafindrakoto, X., Van Oosterhout, R., Santos, C., Mayer, I., & Louwerse, M. (2016). Design for collaboration in mixed reality: Technical challenges and solutions. In *8th International Conference on Games and Virtual Worlds for Serious Applications (VS-GAMES)* (pp. 1–7). Barcelona, Spain.

360VR Porgy and Bess. (2015). Director unknown. The Royal Theatre. Teatro Real, Madrid, Spain. Retrieved from https://www.youtube.com/watch?v=GTU0sil1fBA

Reallusion. (2022). Orpheus VR | re: Naissance Opera Brings Live Virtual Performance with iClone and Motion Capture. Retrieved from https://www.youtube.com/watch?v=ZEsvzHV9-6w

Reed-Danahay, D. (1997). *Auto/ethnography.* New York, NY: Berg.

Renaissance Opera. (2021). OrpheusVR 360 Excerpt: In the Grove. Retrieved from https://www.youtube.com/watch?v=ro9hAzmDgD0

Richardson, N., & Homer. (1974). *The Homeric hymn to Demeter.* Oxford, England: Clarendon Press.

Roesner, D. (2018). Found and framed. A conversation with composer and designer Mathis Nitschke. *Theatre and Performance Design, 4*(3), 204–221. Retrieved from https://doi.org/10.1080/23322551.2018.1523512

Royal Opera House. (2016). Join the Royal Opera Chorus in 360°. Retrieved from https://www.youtube.com/watch?v=gCGO1txNyN8

Royal Swedish Opera. (2020). The Royal Swedish Opera Augmented Reality. Retrieved from https://www.youtube.com/watch?v=OP3gUAfwKAA

Run Lola Run. (Tom Tykwer, 1998). X-Filme Creative Pool Arte Deutschland TV Westdeutscher Rundfunk (WDR) ARTE WDR Fernsehen. Germany.

Ryan, M.-L. (2001). *Narrative as virtual reality: immersion and interactivity in literature and electronic media.* Baltimore, MD: Johns Hopkins University Press.

Schell, J. (2020). *The art of game design: A book of lenses.* Boca Raton, FL: CRC Press.

Shakespeare, W. (2009). *Romeo and Juliet.* Mineola, NY: Dover Publications. (Original work published 1597).

Shakespeare, W. (2002). *Macbeth.* Manhattan, NY: Simon & Schuster. (Original work published 1611).

Shankar, V., Kleijnen, M., Ramanathan, S., Rizley, R., Holland, S., & Morrissey, S. (2016). Mobile shopper marketing: Key issues, current insights, and future research avenues. *Journal of Interactive marketing, 34*(1), 37-48

Sheil, Á., & Vear, C. (2012). Digital opera, new means and new meanings: An Introduction in two voices. *International Journal of Performance Arts and Digital Media, 8*(1), 3–9. https://doi.org/10.1386/padm.8.1.3_2

Silverman, D. (2017). *Doing qualitative research* (5th ed.). Los Angeles, CA: Sage.

Smart, M. (1992). The silencing of Lucia. *Cambridge Opera Journal, 4*(2), 119–141. doi:10.1017/S0954586700003694

Smith, H., & Dean, R. T. (2009). Introduction. In *Practice-led research, research-led practice in the creative arts* (pp. 1–38). Edinburgh, Scotland: Edinburgh University Press. Retrieved from https://www.jstor.org/stable/10.3366/j.ctt1g0b594

Spaniol, M., Klamma, R., Sharda, N., & Jarke, M. (2006). Web-based learning with non-linear multimedia stories. In *Advances in web based learning – ICWL 2006, 4181* (pp. 249–263). Berlin, Germany: Springer Berlin Heidelberg. Retrieved from https://doi.org/10.1007/11925293_23

Spillers, F. (2017). Soundspace: Toward accessible spatial navigation and collaboration for blind users. In *Proceedings of the 5th Symposium on Spatial User Interaction* (pp. 158–158). Retrieved from https://dl.acm.org/doi/pdf/10.1145/3131277.31349 21?casa_token=iLl49Lp8mPQAAAAA%3Aq9wDHle_XuWzAxMaC5BFSTR1 VpcupfZmxMrG-uFh2Lys2-kpEy6T5tBVjeWxWRltKhiXBOH1yGfT

Spotts, F. (1994). *Bayreuth: A History of the Wagner Festival.* Yale University Press. Retrieved from https://books.google.com.au/books?hl=en&lr=&id=mWqXGqaCOE QC&oi=fnd&pg=PR7&dq=Richard+Wagner%27s+construction+of+the+Bayre uth+Theatre&ots=8z1REdPkYb&sig=i3vLnptdiA0fsL_-Z0jYrPUaq_E#v=onep age&q=Richard%20Wagner's%20construction%20of%20the%20Bayreuth%20 Theatre&f=false

St. John Mandel, E. (2014). *Station Eleven.* New York City, NY: Knopf.

Strengell, H. (2003). "You can't kill the goddess": Figures of the goddess Artemis in Stephen King's fiction. *Studies in Popular Culture, 26*(1), 47–64. Retrieved from https://www.jstor.org/stable/pdf/23414987.pdf

Striner, A., Halpin, S., Röggla, T., & César Garcia, P. S. (2021). Towards immersive and social audience experience in remote VR opera. In *IMX '21: Proceedings of the 2021 ACM International Conference on Interactive Media Experiences.* https://doi. org/10.1145/3452918.3465490

Sweet, M. (2015). *Writing interactive music for video games: A composer's guide.* New York City, NY: Pearson Education.

Tykwer, T. (Director). (1998). *Run Lola Run* [Motion picture]. Germany, Arte & Westdeutscher Rundfunk.

Unity Technologies. (2022). *Unity3D* [Computer software]. Retrieved from https:// unity3d.com/get-unity/download

University College London. (2017). MagicFace app. English National Opera. Retrieved from https://dl.acm.org/doi/10.1145/3025453.3025722

Vallance, M., & Towndrow, P. A. (2022). Perspective: Narrative storyliving in virtual reality design. *Frontiers Virtual Reality, 3,* Article 779148. Retrieved from https:// www.frontiersin.org/journals/virtual-reality/articles/10.3389/frvir.2022.779148/full

Van der Aa, M. (2018). *Eight.*

Van Elferen, I. (2016). Analysing game musical immersion: The ALI model. Kingston University. In *Ludomusicology: Approaches to video game music* (pp. 32–52). Sheffield, England: Equinox. Retrieved from https://eprints.kingston.ac.uk/id/eprint/33616/

Vangelis, E. (1994). *Blade Runner Soundtrack.* Atlantic Records, US.

Von Franz, M. L. (1999). *Archetypal dimensions of the psyche.* Boulder, CO: Shambhala Publications.

Visconti. D. (2018). *PermaDeath*

Von Schiller, J. (n.d.). Stanza 19. The Eleusinian Festival. Retrieved from https:// allpoetry.com/The-Eleusinian-Festival

Wagner, R. (1857). *The Ring Cycle.*

Webb, M. (Director). (2009). *(500) Days of Summer* [Motion picture]. United States: Searchlight Pictures, Watermark, Dune Entertainment III.

Welsh National Opera. (2022). Magic Butterfly. Retrieved from https://wno.org.uk/ archive/2017-2018/magic-butterfly

Welsh National Opera. (2017). *Magic Butterfly VR.*

Welsh National Opera. (2019). *A Little Vixen.*

Wilde, O. (1881). *Charmides.* Poems.

Wilde, O. (1994). *Humanitad.* Miscellaneous Poems. Oxford Text Archive Core Collection. Retrieved from https://ota.bodleian.ox.ac.uk/repository/xmlui/handle/20.500.12024/2046

Wilkinson, S., & Appannah, M. (Immersive Storylab). (2020). *Episode 06 – Onboarding/OffBoarding* [Audio podcast]. Retrieved from https://www.spreaker.com/user/brightblack/immersive-storylab-podcast-episode-6-onb_1

Wong, D. (Director). (2021). *Orpheus VR.* [Virtual reality opera performance]. Vancouver, Canada. Re: Naissance Opera.

Worthen, W. B. (2012). "The written troubles of the brain": "Sleep No More" and the space of character. *Theatre Journal (Washington, DC), 64*(1), 79–97. Retrieved from https://doi.org/10.1353/tj.2012.0017

Wurtzler, S. (1992). She sang live, but the microphone was turned off: The live, the recorded, and the *subject* of representation. In R. Altman (Ed.), *Sound theory/sound practice* (pp. 87–103). New York, NY/London: Routledge.

Xenakis, I. (1992). *Formalized music: Thought and mathematics in composition.* Hillsdale, NY: Pendragon Press.

Index

about the author v, xi
acknowledgements xiii
additional tutorial content 2
aim 5 AR opera xvii, 4, 11, 36, 40, 68
AR overlays 36, 66
archetypes 28, 35
artemis 28
assets defined 5
augmented reality i, iii, xv, 9, 12
autoethnography 2, 7

Benyon, D. (2013) 48
broad-brush prototyping 2
Bucher, J. (2018) 42

composer as maker 69–71
composer-designers 2
conceptual framework 5
conclusion 7, 12, 18, 26, 34, 46, 54, 59, 61, 66, 69
context and background 3
creation process 3, 25, 36, 40, 42, 46, 68–70, 72, 73
cyclic artistic process 45
cyclic iterative processes 65, 66
cyclic model 51
cyclic nature of research 6
cyclic reflective process 6
cyclic web 5

design method 54
Dolan Paret's framework for VR storytelling 72

extended reality (XR) 63, 64

female characters in opera 12
feminist opera 28

future work 73

game soundtracks 12
gesamtkunstwerk 12, 13, 44
goddess of hunting 29
goddess of the new moon 31, 32

human-centred design 49
human-computer interaction 48

immersive game sound 12
immersive theatre 7, 9, 12, 15–19, 23, 26, 42, 72, 74, 89, 90, 94
interactive music and games 18–20
introduction 1
iterative process 54

journal entries 55–61

libretto 33, 34

methodology xvii, 1, 6, 9, 41, 46, 48, 53, 71, 75
multisensory experiences 11
music prototyping 3, 51, 63
my journey 75
myths 28, 32–34

narrative design 35, 36, 40–44
new opera 35
non-linear storytelling 24–26
Norman, D. A. (2013) 49

oculus VR 55
onboarding 27, 73
operatic tropes 35
overview xvii

PACT framework 48
performance 1, 4, 9–12, 15–17, 20, 22–24, 26, 27, 36, 37, 43, 44, 48, 49, 66, 71, 73, 74
perspectives 41
practice-based research 6
the producer as composer *versus* the composer as maker 71
prototyping 48, 49, 53, 62–68, 70
psychological archetype 30, 32

reimagining traditional operas 12
relevance and research questions 2
research question 2, 36, 48, 50, 66, 68, 70, 72
review of relevant artworks 14

self-experiential prototyping 46, 48, 50–53, 70
self-experiential prototyping for opera creation 50
site-specific performance 27
software 2, 4, 7, 8, 14, 44, 45, 49, 51, 63
software engineering 48
software processes 66
storyliving 41

thematic context 9
three processes of AR and VR opera creation 72
tilt brush painting software 54
triangulation 5

Unity3D session set-up 45
user experience 48, 49, 68

virtual i, iii, xv, 1–5, 10, 14, 15, 17, 18, 21, 24, 33, 37, 38, 40–45, 50–56, 58, 59, 61–64, 66, 67, 71–74, 89–98
virtual reality opera i, 38
VR storytelling 72

Wagner 13, 15, 44
walkthrough videos 81
women's representation, page 35
world-building 36, 44–46

XR and opera 20–24
XR opera i, ii, xi, xiii, 1, 2, 5, 7, 12, 36, 37, 47, 48, 50, 52, 68, 69, 72, 88, 96
XR production 2, 70

www.ingramcontent.com/pod-product-compliance
Lightning Source LLC
LaVergne TN
LVHW020244020825
817679LV00003B/138

For Product Safety Concerns and Information please contact our EU representative GPSR@taylorandfrancis.com
Taylor & Francis Verlag GmbH, Kaufingerstraße 24, 80331 München, Germany